SOUL PLAY

SOUL PLAY

CONNECTING WITH YOUR SOURCE

SHARON SLOCKBOWER

BALBOA.
PRESS

A DIVISION OF HAY HOUSE

Balboa Press books may be ordered through booksellers or by contacting:

Balboa Press
A Division of Hay House
1663 Liberty Drive
Bloomington, IN 47403
www.balboapress.com
1-(877) 407-4847

Because of the dynamic nature of the Internet, any Web addresses or links contained in this book may have changed since publication and may no longer be valid. The views expressed in this work are solely those of the author and do not necessarily reflect the views of the publisher, and the publisher hereby disclaims any responsibility for them.

The author of this book does not dispense medical advice or prescribe the use of any technique as a form of treatment for physical, emotional, or medical problems without the advice of a physician, either directly or indirectly. The intent of the author is only to offer information of a general nature to help you in your quest for emotional and spiritual well-being. In the event you use any of the information in this book for yourself, which is your constitutional right, the author and the publisher assume no responsibility for your actions.

Any people depicted in stock imagery provided by Thinkstock are models, and such images are being used for illustrative purposes only. Certain stock imagery © Thinkstock.

ISBN: 978-1-4525-3189-2 (sc)
ISBN: 978-1-4525-3191-5 (hc)
ISBN: 978-1-4525-3190-8 (e)

Library of Congress Control Number: 2010919432

Printed in the United States of America

Balboa Press rev. date: 1/26/2011

Acknowledgments

To my husband, my best friend—thank you for supporting me through the good times and the bad. I love you.
To Jenny, Michael, and Laura—when are you moving out?
To my mom and my sisters and my brothers—for a lifetime of memories.
To Cathy—for always listening and loving me anyway.
To all my readers, who made this dream a reality.
And last but certainly not least, to the Source—for your love and guidance, always …

To those readers who wish to contact me, I would love to hear your Soul Play *adventures: SoulPlay1@gmail.com*

Contents

Introduction

What was it that attracted you to pick up this book? Was it the title? The cover? What circumstances in your life do you seek to improve? Are you only recently discovering that you are a spiritual being in addition to the more obvious fact that you are flesh and blood? Or are you already well-versed in spiritual quests and seeking ways to further express the universal teachings of your soul? Would it surprise you to know that you are in control of the circumstances in your life *at this very moment?* Right now, as you hold this book in your hands, you face a pivotal moment. In fact, every time you realize the power of the current moment, you are at a pivotal vantage point simply by being conscious of it. From these realizations, we become active participants in the creation of our futures.

Would it surprise you to know that you can control the circumstances of your life by directing your reactions to them? We all receive and filter impressions from our environment and the events that "occur" to us through our own preconditioned responses. By becoming aware of our reactions and questioning why we feel the way we do toward them, we can redirect and channel our responses and thoughts. These can lead us to greater joy and peace of mind.

For example, when someone makes a hurtful comment or directs anger toward you, the usual response is to feel defensive and to counterattack. What if you realized, in that pivotal moment, that you didn't have to react the way you'd been conditioned? What if you decided that you didn't need to allow the other person's antagonistic attitude to draw you into his or her negativity? What if you could choose, instead, *in that moment,* to maintain inner peace despite the circumstances surrounding you?

I firmly understand that we all, with the Master Creator, co-created the challenges in our lives before our births onto this earth. In fact, all of the circumstances and all of the people in our lives were chosen during this collaboration to give us the opportunity to express the Light within—to demonstrate Love. This book is a tool that will assist you in this mission. It is so easy to forget who we really are ... extensions of God and of one another. We are here to be separated from that knowledge and then to find our way back to it. Once we remember who we are, we become light workers to help others see the divinity that lies within them as well. This happens because, by lifting up first ourselves and then others, we find our joy. Does this knowledge resonate as truth to your soul? If so, you are ready for *Soul Play*! Life need not be dismal—we can create our happiness—beginning *now*.

My spiritual journey began in earnest after a painful separation from my husband, Michael. The need for a separation had been coming for a long time. It seemed, in fact, overdue. But the event hurt tremendously nonetheless. The day after we settled Michael into his new apartment, I sat on our bed at home sobbing so violently that I couldn't catch my breath. I knew I was making myself physically ill, but I felt powerless to stop it. I remembered, somewhere in my desperation, to pray for help. Suddenly I felt an overwhelming presence of Love surround me as I sat there. I felt prompted to run bathwater to soothe my body. As I ran the water, I turned my tear-filled eyes toward a cabinet and again felt a prompting, so I opened the cabinet door. As I did so, a book fell out, and some notes I had taken at the library from an inspirational book, *Living with Joy: Keys to Personal Power and Spiritual Transformation*, by Sanaya Roman, fell out onto the floor. Coincidence? I don't think so. As I read the words and remembered them, I absorbed them from a new perspective—a more receptive perspective. The words of love, truth, and self-empowerment were like a balm to my broken spirit ... an answer to my prayer in a concrete form.

As I focused on restoring and expanding my own energy and withdrew my focus from Michael, I healed. I began to flourish and grow. From this self-accepting and self-loving vantage point, Michael and I were able to re-establish our relationship and eventually re-unite within a healthier marriage. Interestingly, only when I was able to decide to let my marriage end with love and goodwill, that rekindling it became a possibility. Are we both still flawed? You bet! But the way in which we handle our differences has changed.

Our responses and thoughts direct the quality of our lives. This book began as an idea to take beautiful, uplifting words and carry them through the steps of defining and exploring their meaning. As I wrote, I allowed myself to be inspired to include what would be most helpful to you—my reader. I included, with each word, a section entitled "On a personal note," which gives the word more substance in everyday, practical experience. This empowers the reader to see through a window into the life of a fellow traveler on the journey of self-development. The examples I chose, more often than not, reflect imperfections and humor so that the reader can feel comfortable with his or her own shortcomings in the search to grow and learn.

This book focuses on expanding our awareness and living consciously, striving to express our highest vision of ourselves in our daily life. Each essay on these words ends with practical application exercises entitled "Soul Play," which offer readers valuable suggestions for exploring their own inner paths.

I encourage you to enjoy the journey! Spend time on *each* word—a few days, in fact. Don't rush to read through everything at once. The words are listed alphabetically in the table of contents. Choose a word you want to play with:

- Glance through the list, close your eyes, and point to one.
- Open the book to a "random" page and let your soul direct you to a word.
- If you are experiencing a negative energy in your life, think of its direct opposite and choose a word that most closely matches it.
- Meditate quietly and ask to be inspired with a word to focus upon.
- Invite friends or family members who want to expand spiritually to do the exercises together. Watch as the universe gathers events and people around you to bring the energy of the chosen word into reality.
- Keep a journal to write down your experiences as you play and explore. We think we will remember all of the lessons, but this is not usually the case. The journal serves as a reminder for us.

Abundance

Abundance is an overflow of blessings, already present in the universe, waiting for us to attract them toward us. All we need to do is ask, visualize, believe, and focus our attention on appreciating and acknowledging the blessings as they come into our lives.

By asking, we set powers in the universe into motion. Our Source does not interfere with our free will, but waits for us to request that which we want. We must believe that our desires are realistic—that they can become part of our lives. To do this, we must imagine that we already have what we seek. We must visualize the blessing and the results the blessing will bring into our reality. We must do this daily, and not lose faith that we will receive what we want … when the time is right. We must have patience and clarity of intent.

If that for which we ask is not in keeping with our souls' missions here, then the possibility remains that we will not receive. We should always preface our requests with the understanding that we only desire to attract those things that truly benefit our journey. There is a saying, "Be careful of what you wish for or you just may get it." There is wisdom in this. There are times, in retrospect, that we realize that many wonderful coincidences began to happen to draw us toward our destiny, only because our prayers went "unanswered."

When we believe there is a lack—that there are not enough blessings to go around—we become greedy and possessive. This false paradigm of lack creates fear and repels the very blessings we seek. Abundance is an overflow—there is no lack in the universe. What is available to you is available to all. Like love, we must open a conduit to give as well as to receive. This keeps the flow of blessings from stagnating.

On a personal note:

There was a night last autumn when my daughter Laura and I were walking the mile from my mother's house to the beach. Night had fallen, and the air was crisp and clear. The stars seemed close enough to pull down from the sky. As we reached the deserted boardwalk, I could hear the rhythmic pounding of the surf and taste the salt in the air. We lay back on the sand for a comfortable view of the stars—not caring that it would take an hour to get it out of our hair—and just absorbed the moment.

I felt such a deep, contented peace, so grateful for the beauty of the place, and the company of my daughter (now nineteen years old and human again). I decided, in that moment, that I wanted my life to be an example of abundance. I wanted to appreciate every nuance of my journey here and to surround myself with beauty and light.

There is opportunity to appreciate abundance in every situation. I find that even at my worst moments, if I take the time to look, I will discover something to be grateful for. When I do this, my focus changes, and the universe responds … sending more of those things I pay attention to.

Even in the most difficult of times, we can appreciate something. I learned this important lesson from one of my patients. He was a young man in his early forties, and he came to us through hospice, a service provided for those who are dying. He had been an alcoholic and his liver was not functioning, causing poisons to build up in his body. His skin was as yellow and waxy as banana peels. I learned from his best friend that he'd been an avid surfer and loved the sun and the sea. I looked at the shell of a man in the bed, shivering even with several blankets over him. It was summer, and I thought of the many months he'd been in the hospital, deprived of the abundance of nature, missing the rejuvenation of life returning with the spring. I made the decision to get him outside on the first sunny day.

I brought him a CD of soothing music with the sound of ocean waves in the background. We wheeled him out on a lounge chair and placed him in the warmth of the sun. I will never forget the look in his eyes. Surrounded by jaundiced yellow were the bluest eyes imaginable holding a spark of life, where moments before, they were dull with the anticipation of death. He turned his face toward the sun, and although he could no longer speak, I could see the appreciation in his countenance. Even in a moment such as this, it is possible to receive abundance.

We are not promised an easy life, but we can have an abundant one if we focus our attention on the positive and refuse to dwell on the negative. As we attract those things we focus our attention upon, it only makes sense to spend more time thinking about things that bring us joy.

Soul play:

- Spend some time thinking about which blessings you want to bring into your life. Do you believe this blessing is realistic? Can you visualize yourself living with this blessing?
- Don't forget to ask! Often we wish we could have something in our lives, but we forget to ask our Source for assistance. State your intentions in a clear and concise manner.
- Devote ten or fifteen minutes each day (preferably after you rise) sitting quietly and imagining the blessings unfolding in your life.
- Determine that your life will be a living example of abundance—spiritual, emotional, and material—let your cup run over, and allow the overflow to nourish others. Become a conduit for abundance—receiving and giving—and the blessings will flow.
- When times are difficult, seek out the positive. Look for hidden blessings. Recognize your blessings as you receive them. Keep your eyes open!

Adventure

Adventure is an exhilarating experience that usually requires us to take risks. It stretches our imagination and lifts us out of the routines and existence we are used to.

This entire lifetime is an adventure! We decided to come to this Earth knowing the multitude of dangers, sorrows, and darkness we would find here, excited to experience it all and to learn. Life is similar to an amusement park ride, with exhilarating highs, belly-sinking lows, and hold-your-breath moments. It is up to us to decide if we experience it with white-knuckled fear or screams of excitement!

We are continually presented with choices that will lead us down one path or another. Deciding to make changes or take risks is necessary to set out on an adventure. Yet fearing change often deters us from doing so. We decide that "the devil we know is better than the devil we don't know," and we continue on with situations out of fear of the unknown.

Trust is needed in order to embrace and enjoy the adventure. We have the choice to look upon the butterflies in our stomachs as excitement instead of fear and laugh as they tickle us. We can choose to jump into the adventure with both feet, ready to embrace the highs and lows, open to learning from both. We can trust that, even when we fall, there is a safety net ready to catch us. Go for it!

On a personal note:

At 4:00 AM one morning, I got a frantic phone call from the administrator of the nursing home I was working with at the time—the facility was actively flooding as a result of Hurricane Floyd the previous day. I threw on my clothes, jumped into my car, and realized, to my dismay, that nearly all the roads I needed to take were flooded and roadblocks had been set up everywhere. Through the assistance of some Godsent people, I managed to find my way to work and began the surrealistic job of bringing residents and medical records to safety.

As a result of the flood, extensive repairs and renovations were necessary, and the residents were sent to "sister" facilities. Our staff was temporarily sent to those facilities to facilitate the process while the renovations began on our building. It was an hour commute to the new nursing homes, and several of the nurses carpooled. On the way home one evening, about a month after the flood, we were discussing the probability that the company would be laying off staff until the renovations were complete. Several nurses were worried about what to do and where they would work. I felt the butterflies in my stomach as well, but I chose to look at them as excitement. I cheered the nurses on by reminding them of all the times they complained about their jobs, and told them to look at it as an open opportunity to move into something great. The mood in the car changed.

There was one sister facility that was having a difficult time with the transition of accepting all the new residents and staff, and I was sent to smooth things over. I met with the director of nursing, and we developed a good working relationship. She was leaving to accept a position in another nursing home and asked me to come with her, so I jumped on the opportunity, and the adventure brought me to a place I have come to love.

I could have agonized over the chaos that the flood brought and put my head under the covers, gone on unemployment until the facility reopened, or chose any number of change-avoiding choices. But by looking upon those butterflies as excitement instead of fear, I accepted the adventure of life and plunged in.

Adventure doesn't have to come in the form of major life changes, though. Simply getting into the car to go somewhere you haven't been before can be an adventure. So can taking a class to learn a new subject, going to a party where you don't know anyone, or going for a walk in the woods and taking a path you never took before—all sorts of opportunities surround us! All we have to do is look for one and embark upon the journey.

Don't wait for a hurricane to shake you loose from a situation or job you are unhappy with. Don't stay with the devil you know because you fear the unknown. Be willing to take a risk and stop settling for less than you want out of life.

Soul play:

- Consider which changes you have been afraid to make. Determine if the devil-you-know viewpoint has prevented you from making the changes you need to create the opportunity to be happier.
- If fear was not an issue, what would you have done differently up to now?
- How can looking upon change with excitement realign your perspective?
- How can trust assist you in taking risk and embracing the unknown?
- Practice taking small risks, and feel the exhilaration and freedom you feel from having felt the fear and pushed through it.
- Grab a map or go online and choose a place you've never been before. Choose something that sounds exciting or different. Plot out your directions and just go! You can pick a friend who wants to join in the adventure, or plan the adventure together. Or go alone!
- Call your local community college as ask for a list of available night classes. Pick something you've always been interested in learning more about and sign up for the class.

Balance

Balance is the proportioning of our activities and attention, which results in greater harmony in our lives. It is a pleasing arrangement of our focus and time to create internal calm and decrease our inner conflict.

First, we must examine what is important to us—family, friends, home, health, recreation, learning, work, spiritual nourishment, and so on. We can review the recent past to determine how much attention we have devoted to each of these aspects of our life and to decide whether we have focused more on one to the detriment of another. If we have felt internal discord or experienced more conflict and dissatisfaction recently, chances are good that there has been an imbalance.

It is tempting, when problems arise due to imbalance, to place blame on outside forces. This is a false belief that disempowers us. We are responsible for our own choices. For our own reasons, we chose to focus on one area over another. It is for us to evaluate those reasons and decide whether they were valid enough to risk the consequences.

We cannot wait for a vacation to change imbalances. It is a dangerous misperception to believe we can "make up" for lost time. Today is all there really is, and it is today that counts. If enough todays pass by with imbalanced attention to important areas of life, they will atrophy. It will not matter that we are now focusing attention on them, because they will be too weak to respond. This applies not only to our health but to our relationships (two of the most important aspects of our lives, which are often attended to last).

When we achieve balance and coordinate our daily routines to encompass all of what is important, the results are immediate. There is inner peace, improvement in relationships, greater health, and more joy and appreciation for life.

On a personal note:

I am quite familiar with the juggling routine—trying to fit everything into a twenty-four hour span and still wind up with a few hours' sleep each night can be challenging. There's the commute to work, putting in at least eight (usually more) work hours, keeping up with the housework, spending quality time with loved ones, finding time for ourselves and for exercise—which is always the last thing I consider when it should be the first!

So where do we find the time to fit everything in? Well, point blank—we can't. The current society and fiscal climate is such that at least two incomes are necessary in our household. Funny, isn't it, that the old full-time job, reminiscent of the 1950s "homemaker and mother," must now be crammed into our so-called spare time in the evening. Sorry, but I'm just not that ambitious! So something had to give! And it wasn't going to be my sanity.

My solution (and we each must find our own) was an all-hands-on-deck approach. If everybody pitches in, it isn't impossible. Anyone with two hands is eligible. Make a list of household chores that must be done or you would die if someone knocked on your door to visit. Decide to live with whatever can't be done within an hour. Everyone's priorities are different; a spotless home is not high on my list. I'd rather take the time to lie on my bed with my daughter and talk about her day while we scratch each other's backs.

I use every bit of downtime I get. I read magazines on line at the store, listen to inspirational music or authors while driving to work, or read a good book while I'm in the waiting room at the doctor's office. I like to prepare for downtime whenever possible, so I can make the most of it. It prevents me from getting aggravated and impatient when I have to wait.

I know I spend too much time on recreational TV—mindless sitcoms, watching a movie I've seen before (that's two hours of useless time!), the many minutes flicking around the channels to decide what I want to watch. This is my area of attack if I want to find time to devote to improving the imbalance in my life. Where is yours? If you can't identify an area of excess, and your schedule is jam-packed, something's got to go if it is negatively impacting other, more important, aspects of your life.

Soul play:

+ Write down areas of life that are important to you. Try not to leave anything out.

+ Review the past week. Write down what percent of your time you devoted to each area. Include everything! Don't forget sleep time. If you simply can't guesstimate, then take a week to chronicle your time so that you can get a better idea of where you're spending it. (It's a lot like creating a budget or starting a diet and journaling what you eat!)

+ Has your life been harmonious as a result of your distribution of attention to the various areas of your life? What hasn't been working? What part of your life is showing signs of being out of balance?

+ Consider restructuring your priorities and the time you spend focusing on them. After you have determined where your time and energy has been going each day, decide to take control of your schedule so you can arrange your day according to your priorities. Work and travel time are first, if you must financially support your family. You know how much sleep you require to avoid crankiness—block out this time as well. Take the remaining hours and prioritize them according to those areas of life most important to you. If you do this, and your highest priority is family relationships, be prepared and accepting that your house may not be spotless, but be thankful that your relationships will flourish.

+ Be aware of how your day is spent—if you are taking too much time at work talking with friends about issues not related to the job at hand, the workday will be longer (or your productivity will suffer). Time at work spent on things other than "work" cannot be considered in your eight-hour work slot. This time must be chronicled in a category for "relationships with friends." Otherwise, you will feel deprived at the end of a nine- or ten-hour workday that you didn't have time left for your home, family and friends, when in actuality, an hour or more was devoted to listening to your friends discuss their weekends.

Beauty

Beauty is something that brings joy and appreciation to the observer. As each individual perspective is diverse, there can be no universal definition of beauty.

The focus on the quest for beauty in our lives requires a redirection of our attention from what others define as beauteous to discovering what brings us joy and appreciation. Amazingly, there are many who have not given themselves the gift of exploring this definition. The world has conditioned us to believe that to surround oneself with beauty is to acquire things—a home of a particular size, in a particular neighborhood, with a spouse who looks and acts in a particular manner, with clothing of a particular brand, and a car of a particular make and model.

We have become so used to being told what is beautiful that we have given up our own freedom and divine need to discover for ourselves what brings us joy. This is why so many who have so much are still not happy. They are not content with their lives and are always searching to fill the gap with "things." They have not discovered their own sense of beauty. They have not yet learned that there is beauty to be found in all things.

The true challenge is not to seek beauty but to recognize it within everything around us. There is no lack, no void to fill. We can open our spiritual eyes and observe the world from that perspective. We can look upon the face of the old woman and see the beauty of her wrinkles—each one formed by years of experiences and living. We can look upon the riotous magnificence of an untamed garden rather than a manicured lawn and revel in its unique beauty. We can look at ourselves in the mirror and appreciate our own reflection exactly as it is.

On a personal note:

I feel such sadness sometimes when I watch the extreme makeover shows on TV. It isn't so much the fact that these people undergo major surgery to improve themselves that bothers me but that they have allowed other people to make them feel so ugly in their own skin.

I remember how awful that feels. Somewhere around puberty, when I was caught between feeling self-conscious and more self-conscious, I began to break out in psoriasis. We're not talking about the little patch on the elbows here ... we're talking about the head-to-toe variety. Now take this preteen and add some extra poundage to the mix ... get the picture?

Children can be cruel, and they were. Doctors were just as bad. One sadistic doctor decided to experiment on me by forcing me to wear one of those hard plastic sweat suits (do they even still make them?) to bed at night. Worse, I had to slather myself first with ointment that smelled like tar. Just imagine wearing this contraption—smelly goop under a plastic suit from the neck down—in August without air conditioning. Needless to say, I didn't sleep much. Other girls were out buying pretty nightgowns, and I smelled like a freshly paved driveway!

I bought into the idea that I wasn't pretty. I did not meet the world's criteria for beauty. This devastated me. After all, just a few years before, wasn't I the skinny little girl with long blonde hair and bright blue eyes people predicted would be a "heartbreaker"? Wasn't I the same child who would spend hours in front of the mirror trying on clothes and sneaking into my mother's makeup drawer to try on lipstick? Wasn't I the same person who would put on her lacy hat and gloves to wear to church and feel like a princess?

I learned, very clearly, that the world treats you differently when you are not pretty. At first, this knowledge was difficult to take. I believed I was worthless. But from the depths of this despair, true beauty was created. Compassion was born. Sensitivity was developed. Strength of character was forged. I became beautiful inside. This kind of beauty does not fade when time wrinkles the skin. I came to appreciate that getting psoriasis might have been a gift rather than a curse.

We don't have to wait until we have plastic surgery or lose thirty pounds to feel beautiful. Self love is the most powerful beauty makeover there is. When someone loves and respects herself or himself, regardless of the skin they are in, it creates an energy that draws others to appreciate his or her uniqueness. Have you ever met someone who gets more attractive the longer you talk to him or her? Chances are, that person is confident about their own beauty.

We have to stop looking in the mirror for our flaws and seek instead to build ourselves up in our own eyes. Instead of seeing that new wrinkle, notice the sparkle in your eye! We have the power to exude true beauty!

Soul play:

+ What do you find beautiful? Why? Determine if this value judgment is your own or imposed upon you by others.
+ Stand in front of your mirror. Look for your own beauty. Suspend negativity and look only for what you can appreciate. Even if you can only bring yourself to find one compliment, tell yourself—out loud— about your own beauty. Don't stop with what you see on the outside, tell yourself about all of your inner qualities as well.
+ Choose something you have considered to lack beauty ... open your mind to viewing it differently. Put aside the judgment of the world. What beauty can you see now, when you are looking for it?
+ Surround yourself with reminders of your own beauty. Make an index card listing your qualities. Keep it in your pocket. Pull it out when you're on line at the store or stuck at a red light. Remind yourself continually to remember your own beauty, and you will become more beautiful.

Birth

Birth is the process of bringing creation into reality. We give birth, as it were, to ideas, thoughts, actions, beliefs, hopes, dreams, and so on. Birth is the physical manifestation of our creation … the spoken word, the dream becoming reality, the acting out from a belief, the written thought, the painted image …

We are co-creators with our Source, and it is in our divine nature to seek to create. Often there is in one's life a desire to manifest a long-cherished dream, and we find our "spiritual clocks" ticking. Go with this instinct! Our soul knows when its time has come!

The conception of the highest idea should be sought in this process. As in gestation, there is much work to be done before the birth. The formation of that which is to be born requires careful nurturing to produce the highest outcome. Everything we absorb from the world around us will have an impact. We can surround ourselves with beauty and light. Listen to inspiring music; read words that uplift and expand the mind. Commune with nature … invite positive people to spend time with us. We can focus our thoughts on the good in all things. As in gestation, we can keep our vessel healthy to provide the best conduit for creativity: eating foods produced by nature, drinking plenty of water to lubricate the cells, and exercising the body. These things will feed your creation!

Just as with the birth of a child, the process of birthing a creation can be fearful. Will it be healthy? Will I be able to take care of and nurture it? Will others find it as beautiful as I do? What will become of it? What if I don't finish it? The list of worries can be daunting. Patience, strength, endurance, faith, and courage are required … but the results are always rewarding.

On a personal note:

It has been a dream of mine to write a book since I was young. At first, I thought it would be a romance novel, or a mystery, or something of that sort.

But as I got older and began to seek enlightenment of a spiritual nature, I developed an almost palpable need to write something that would help bring light into the world.

This need grew over time, and although my schedule continued to be hectic and fast-paced, my spiritual clock was ticking. I knew it was time to give birth to this book. But the question was how? When? Should I do it after working ten hours and commuting home an hour? How could I possibly manage it?

When I decided to focus on why and how I could manage it, and sought assistance from a higher Source, the ideas flowed. I chose early morning, when the house was quiet and I could meditate and open myself up to be inspired. Before bed, I chose a word to write about so that in the morning my mind could have mulled over it. As I showered for the day, the time was used to brainstorm ideas.

The birthing of this book began the day I decided it could be done. It began the moment I believed this could become a reality. During the "gestation" period, I came to understand that when I surrounded myself with things that inspired me, my process was easy and joyful. The flow of ideas came quickly. I knew I was co-creating with the Source, and this brought such a feeling of excitement and fulfillment to me. I was finally doing what I had always dreamed, always known, I was meant to do.

There have been times I have not felt as inspired. Times when the words did not flow, and the birthing process was stalled. I would become impatient, doubt my ability to handle my schedule, worry that the flow of ideas would cease, have a few glasses of wine to "unwind" from a hectic day, and hit the snooze button on my alarm clock so many times that I left no time to write. I learned that these were the things that killed my creativity. These lessons were vitally important.

I also realized that after I had visited with someone who was positive and passionate about life, I was energized. If I spent the day at the library filling my mind and spirit with words of truth and light, my batteries were charged! When I took the time to go for a walk in the woods, I felt at peace and physically de-stressed. If I drank water instead of wine, I woke up refreshed and ready to write.

The same lessons can benefit you, whether you are birthing a painting or designing a home, or thinking of ways to be a better parent, or writing a song, or creating a business ... just don't get caught up in reasons why something can't be manifested! Get caught up in the excitement of the process of creation! Stop worrying about the end results and go for it!

Soul play:

- What idea or dream have you wanted to create and birth into reality?
- Write your idea or dream on a page in your journal. Next to it, write all the reasons why it is important for you to create.
- Next, write down things you can do today, right now, to begin birthing the idea into a reality. For example, if you want to create a painting, do you have paints and a paintbrush? A canvas? Right now, get into your car and drive to the store to purchase your supplies.
- Write the names of people who inspire you. Call them and make plans to go for a walk together, or meet for dinner. Share your ideas with them.
- Take a few moments each morning to meditate on the thing you wish to create. Invite the Source to join your meditation and ask for assistance with ideas to develop a plan to make your dream a reality.
- What (or who) drains your energy? Avoid it or them while you are gestating!
- Enjoy yourself! Stop being so serious, or worried about success! Your creation will be beautiful because it is yours ... it may not be perfect, but this is okay!
- Congratulate yourself after the birth of your idea and, as always, give thanks.

Clarity

Clarity is the ability to perceive reality through the lens of truth. It is obtaining insight into people and situations—past, present, and future. It is the ability to see what deeper meaning is waiting to be observed, so that we might make better choices to achieve our soul's mission or assist others with theirs.

Make no mistake—all events and people we encounter are not coincidental. All are destined to teach us something. It is our responsibility to become aware in the moment, to have our camera loaded and ready to focus upon what we are supposed to learn. There is no auto-focus on this camera! There must be conscious intent and desire for clarity.

But first, some preparation is required to clean the lens. Our lenses are the view through which we see the world. They become soiled by prejudices, the beliefs of others, past experiences, and so on. We need to evaluate what is distorting our lens. Once we establish this, the work of cleansing begins.

Love is the basic cleansing solvent—we can add a touch of understanding, humor, forgiveness, or whatever is needed into the mixture. It is also important for the inner workings of the camera to be in order. In terms of the body, taking in toxins (this includes alcohol, harmful drugs, smoke, negative thinking, and so on) will influence the ability to focus with clarity. When ingesting such toxins, our insights become clouded.

Having removed the distortions of our lenses, and cleansed the "camera" of toxins, we are ready to take the picture. Focus on the situation, see the characters and surrounding events, evaluate what the lesson might be from the moment and snap the image. Reflect upon this image at the end of the day when things are quiet, and evaluate the insights provided by it. Imprint the moment into memory so that in the future the image can be drawn upon in order to remind us of the wisdom it provided.

On a personal note:

It is so easy to go through life with blinders on. We are so busy and preoccupied that we miss what's right in front of our faces most of the time. There are countless opportunities to learn and to express love that cross our paths every day, a thousand "coincidences" we don't recognize, and we are so concerned with getting from point A to point B that we breeze right by them!

When I make a deliberate effort to connect with the events that unfold in my day and learn from them, my lens opens, and I see so much more than I would otherwise. I pick up on subtle clues. I notice the people around me. I look at body language, observe responses—my own and others'—and try to determine what motivates each of us. I find that I learn the most from the people I least want to interact with!

On one of those days, when I had decided to "live consciously in the moment" (I make this commitment on a regular basis, but then all kinds of chaos in my schedule interferes!), a particularly cranky, negative patient came up to me at the nurses' station while I was trying to do at least ten other things. While I was in the middle of typing on the computer, speaking into the phone, gesturing to the nursing assistants to pass the lunch trays that had just arrived on the unit, and using one foot to open a drawer to obtain a file, this woman began yelling at me at the top of her lungs. The chosen topic of the moment (and there were as many as her imagination could conjure) consisted of being insulted that she had been offered a shower. Even though I held up a finger to request a moment to finish the phone conversation, she continued her tirade, creating a scene at the desk. I apologized to the family member on the phone, promising to return the call later, and turned to give my attention to my tormentor.

I could feel my annoyance as a palpable thing … the redness crept onto my face as other residents turned to watch her holler at me. Then in a flash, I remembered my commitment to myself to be conscious of the moment. I "cleansed my lens" of annoyance and frustration and simply observed.

Standing in front of me, pointing a finger gnarled with painful arthritis was a white-haired, stooped-over elderly woman holding onto the desk with her other hand to support herself while she yelled. Her blue eyes sparkled with indignation, and her cheeks were slightly red with excitement. I observed that her cheekbones were high and fine, and realized that she must have been quite pretty in her youth. I listened to the words she yelled—she'd obviously been insulted by the offer of the shower.

And I had a moment of clarity. I understood.

This woman was tormented by the knowledge that she could not shower herself without assistance. This woman—once a beautiful, vital, and productive wife, mother, daughter, homemaker, lover—could not even clean herself any longer, and she was coping with the only power she had left—her voice. This clarity, this wisdom, helped me soothe this woman on a deeper level. It helped me plan her care in ways that would provide the least injury to her pride. It allowed me to share my insights with other staff members so they could be more understanding of her behaviors. Then later, when confronted with similar situations, I could take the wisdom learned from that photographic moment and use it to comfort someone else. When provided with this sensitivity, the staff was able to shower the resident and provide hygiene with dignity.

Soul play:

- Decide to live a day "conscious in the moment." If a day is too long to start with, try an hour, or the next ten minutes.
- Observe who crosses your path and their body language. Listen to them.
- Ask yourself, "What am I meant to learn from this interaction?" and "How can I use this wisdom?"
- Consider a situation in which insight is or was lacking. What was distorting your lens? What continues to distort your lens?
- Decide which cleaning agents you need to clean your lens and practice it (remember, love is the basic ingredient!).
- Refocus on the situation with clarity now. What insights have you received? Write them in your journal so you can reflect on them again in the future.

Communication

Communication is the process of sharing an understanding of thoughts, feelings, and information with another. This can be accomplished in several ways: through a written message, the words we speak, body language, and even telepathy.

Clear communication promotes respect and paves the path of progress. Failure to give and receive a clear message results in arguments, frustration, anger, hurt feelings, misperceptions, loss of relationships, and so on. This is why it is essential to place importance on the message we are receiving. We cannot assume we will always receive the message correctly. Sometimes we become defensive based on the way we incorrectly interpret messages. Even culturally, the way speech is delivered can be abrupt, and another culture may not understand that no offense was intended. When this happens, misunderstandings may occur and antagonistic feelings follow.

We also must not assume our message is more important than the other person's. We must avoid assuming what the other person will say as well. To do so leads to closing off communication—after all, why bother listening when we already know what is going to be said? If we are not actively listening, we might misunderstand what is being communicated.

Active listening involves recognition that the person before us deserves our focused attention. We must give this person our undivided attention, without distraction. This demonstrates respect and a desire to understand, and it opens a conduit—a pathway—for communication to flow.

Observe what is unsaid as well as what is spoken. What does the other person's body language and facial expressions say about underlying feelings? Ask them if the impressions you are receiving are accurate. Don't assume that because the other person is frowning, they are angry. Ask!

Do not become distracted by focusing on formulating a response, or by trying to persuade the other that your viewpoint is correct. There will be time for that later. First, seek to understand! Ask questions, repeat your perception of what was just communicated, and allow the other to clarify any parts of the message you did not receive fully or correctly.

When it is agreed with the other person that we understand all aspects of the message he or she wished to communicate, it is our turn. Request that the other demonstrate the same respect and attention he or she received. Encourage questions. We should avoid expressing our message in a way that places blame or criticism upon the other as this will block the flow of communication by causing the other to become defensive. We can express our feelings without accusing the other. We are responsible for our own feelings and must not blame the other person for having caused them.

When an understanding of each other's message is complete, seek common grounds—areas of agreement—and expand upon these. Agree to disagree when necessary and respect each other's right to express our own views. Often, just knowing the other person understands our viewpoint (even if they disagree) goes a long way in resolving issues through clear communication.

On a personal note:

In the healthcare field, I have worked with a variety of individuals with differing cultures, backgrounds, beliefs, religions, mannerisms, and even speech patterns. It is a microcosm of the world—with people from Jamaica, Africa, the Philippines, Israel, Russia, Haiti, Ghana—you name it. I have had the privilege of getting to know these interesting people. I have also witnessed the discord that can result from different cultures clashing, and the misunderstandings and hurt feelings that can develop when there is a lack of communication.

Without understanding the background of an individual, we cannot accurately interpret the meaning behind the spoken word. For example, my sister, Marion, is a very blunt, honest, and in-your-face type of person. We never need to wonder what she is thinking. Everyone who knows Marion understands that she has a heart of pure gold and not a mean bone in her body. I find her personality refreshing and enjoyable. But someone who does not know her could be offended by her honesty. Not knowing that she would give the shirt off her back, someone might misinterpret her intent.

I see this kind of misunderstanding in the workplace as well. In the African culture, a request for assistance might be worded crisply as, "Come help me," whereas a Filipino person's request might be worded more softly as, "Could you please assist me, madam?" This does not mean the African's request is better or worse—it is just interpreted differently by the listener based upon their backgrounds. Whereas someone from the Philippines may feel the request to "come help me" was rudely phrased, another person from Africa would not think there was anything wrong with the way the request was made. Therefore, the problem develops not because the message was wrongly delivered, but because it was received defensively, correctly or not. We must make an attempt to understand the intent of the person speaking before we choose to take issue with what was said.

The one decisive similarity in all mankind is that we all share the same feelings. Everyone knows what it is like to feel angry, sad, frustrated, hurt, resentful, happy, peaceful, loving, and so on. Our cultures or family backgrounds can determine which events evoke these emotions. People process events differently, and we cannot expect that everyone will feel the same about every circumstance. But we can focus on the feelings. These we have in common. If we know our actions are causing hurt feelings in another, even if we don't agree the other person should have responded the way he or she did, perhaps we can change the way we act to prevent hurting or insulting the other. Or perhaps we are taking offense at another's actions when no offense was intended, and with the new understanding that no harm was intended, can we choose to accept the differences without feeling insulted?

Soul play:

+ Have you been upset by or felt resentful toward the actions or beliefs of another person? What actions or words have you objected to? Write them down in a way that focuses on your feelings and does not blame the other person for causing them.
+ Meet with the other person and follow the guidelines listed to communicate these feelings and thoughts. Focus on listening and understanding the other's view.

Compassion

Compassion is the selfless act of identifying with the energy of another while he or she is experiencing an event in his or her life perceived as painful or fearful. It is the sharing of "passion" with another. This sharing does not necessarily have to involve negativity. It can also be the sharing of passion for something joyful.

It is necessary to use care when deciding to empathize with another while that person is in a negative state of mind and/or heart. Remember, the purpose of compassion is to comfort the other so he or she does not feel alone in this moment of pain. It is to reassure the person that someone understands how he or she is feeling. Once this communion has been established, the work of raising the energies begins. This is a delicate process that requires all parties to participate.

Acknowledge the pain or fear, uncover its source, discuss which beliefs the other has to determine why the event should have elicited negative responses, and invite the person to determine what conditioning in his or her life has led to the belief that this is the only appropriate response. Remind the person how loved he or she really is, and that he or she is connected to a Source of love so great in its power that any obstacle can be overcome. Finally, invite the other person to meditate upon a new response to the situation. Ask him or her to bring the light of the Source into the new response and to allow the release, which forgiveness of self or others will bring.

If the other is resistant at any stage of this healing, do not become frustrated with him or her. This person may not be ready yet to receive the light. Send love—it will be there when he or she is open to it. Finally—and this is essential—remember to keep your own energy raised. Focus on love and consciously let go of the negative communion, even if the other is attempting to bring you down. It serves the other person no useful purpose to continue to focus on pain or fear. You do the other no good by continued attention to these responses.

It is not a lack of kindness to climb out of the pit of despair as long as the other is aware that you are holding a rope to assist him or her into the light when he or she is ready.

On a personal note:

I have spent a great many hours in the company of those experiencing pain and fear. I must have been given the gift of empathy, because I am sensitive to the thoughts and feelings of those around me. This has also been a curse at times, because I have absorbed those energies without knowing how to redirect and recover from them. It is true that I offered those who were suffering a willing ear to listen to their sorrow, and a shoulder to cry on, but in the end … did I help them as much as I could have? Or did I just manage to lower my own energy so they didn't feel alone? There were times I would feel awful that I hadn't managed to "cheer them up."

I have learned that in order to help someone through to the other side of fear and pain, all I can do is show him or her the map. The other person is responsible for his or her own journey. I also came to understand that once the person had a chance to vent his or her upset, it only worsened the other's state to continue to rehash the thing over and over. This only serves to reinforce the negativity.

I also discovered that when I began to pull back my energy after having attempted to raise that of the other, I often encountered resistance. The person wanted me to remain in misery too. In the beginning, I would feel guilty about not giving in to this. But I knew that we get what we focus upon, and that to continue to commiserate would not be helping. Only love and forgiveness heals.

Soul play:

+ Open your eyes to the pain of another. Actively seek out those who are suffering and need compassion.
+ Make a point to listen to and understand the other's feelings about the triggering event or situation. Ask questions.

- Open your heart to commune with their feelings, and empathize with the hurt they are feeling. Hold the others in your arms and give comfort and love.

- Only after all of the above has been accomplished, begin to explore why the other sees pain as the only response to the situation. Attempt to explore alternatives, and remind the other of his or her connection to Source.

- Respect the other's choice if he or she is unwilling or not ready to release the pain, and send them love.

Courage

Courage is being afraid of consequences but acting upon our values and hopes *in spite* of the dangers or worries. It is the giving of permission to open ourselves to emotional, financial, social, political, or physical harm in the interest of doing what we believe is the right thing.

When we choose to be courageous, we embrace and overcome our fears. Fear is an absence of trust in the universe and in ourselves to provide what we need. When we understand that the universe always provides what we need, on a soul level, it becomes easier to release fear.

We may experience consequences after acting upon our values. This is an inevitable risk and fact of life. The consequences may be exactly what we need for our growth. When compared with the feelings of paralysis and helplessness that arise from not acting courageously, these consequences are more palatable.

Regret for inaction and the damage to self-esteem that occurs by giving in to fear can consume us and render us powerless. Conversely, choosing to work past the fear and act upon our integrity creates energy and fills us with a sense of empowerment. This invariably raises our self-esteem.

We all live primarily in our comfort zones, where life is unchanging and safe. When we anticipate a change on the horizon, it is tempting to anticipate all the negative occurrences that might be impending. We do not have to paralyze ourselves with such thoughts. We can choose instead to anticipate and focus on the growth factor and on what positive results could manifest. Change is a fact of life. This fact doesn't cease because we live in fear of it. If we choose, instead, to embrace change—to become excited by the adventure of it—we create the energy we need to live courageously and to be happy.

On a personal note:

When I think of courage and standing up for what is right, I think of people like Martin Luther King Jr. To knowingly risk personal safety in order to fight injustice, even though it is a fearful thing, epitomizes courage to me. I'm sure it was not a comfortable thing for this man to worry that every time he opened his door, he was a target for some racist nut-job. But, in spite of this fear, and maybe because of it, he was driven to radically change the way the country was unjustly operating. Yes, his outcome was the loss of his life—but look at the other outcomes. Nearly half a century later, the country is a different, better place because he lived courageously. Granted, the world and the people in it are not perfect, but acceptance of racial equality has improved dramatically because of people like Dr. King. Imagine how different the country would be now if men like this had chosen inaction in the face of injustice.

Most of us aren't presented with such dramatic opportunities to stand up for justice in our lives. But what we do with the more humble moments count too. In my high school, there was a girl who was picked on by the "popular" crowd. She was shy and never stood up for herself when they did this. I was a little shy myself, and not one given to standing out in the crowd but was content to sit in the middle with my handful of friends and go unnoticed. One day after a filmstrip ended, one of the popular girls started to tease their usual prey, and like a pack of jackals they were soon tormenting her to the point of making her cry. I suddenly couldn't take it anymore, ashamed I had not spoken up before, and began to publicly berate them for their behavior. The whole class hushed while I told these girls how rotten they were acting, and I could see everyone's surprise that I had done so. When I was finished, there was no clapping like in the movies. No one patted me on the back to say, "It's about time someone told those jerks off!" The girl I'd defended never said, "Thank you."

The bell rang and everyone went to their next class. I'd risked being a social outcast to stand up against injustice, and no one had noticed! But what was great was that it didn't matter to me what the others thought; I was proud of myself for having had the courage to take a risk and stand up for what was right.

Often just handling the circumstances of our lives can reflect courage. I took my father-in-law for his chemotherapy treatment the other day. We went to an outpatient office, where a disturbingly huge number of patients receive chemotherapeutic agents in an assembly line-type setting. The chairs were lined up in a long row and were full of people coping with a deadly diagnosis. As the afternoon wound down, the seats were emptying, and a woman walked in. You know how some people walk into a room and own it? She had a huge smile on her face, and she went around wishing everyone a happy new year and hugged the nurses. She was wearing a business suit, and exuded an aura of self-confidence and good cheer. I assumed she was the office manager, and I was shocked when she took off her jacket and placed it around the back of one of the chairs to get ready for her chemo treatment! This woman was faced with the loss of her life, and she greeted the room with enthusiasm and warmth. To me, this woman was the embodiment of courage!

Soul play:

- Identify an area of your life where change or a decision about following a different course of action is necessary. What are your highest visions regarding this change? Determine if you have feelings of fear over possible consequences. Do you perceive a lack of trust in your ability to handle whatever consequences arise? Consider a worst-case scenario and envision yourself handling the consequences with dignity, a sense of humor, and confidence. Say to yourself, "I can handle this." Set your mind toward positive action.

- If you feel fear, examine it. Determine why you feel this way. Is it based on realistic information? How can pushing through it, with action, empower you? Make the decision to act! Step out of your comfort zone.

- If you feel something is unjust, stand up for what you believe in and express your higher truths.

Creativity

Creativity is the gift of manifesting one's vision into the world through intention. When we are in the act of creation, we are expressing the power of our Source. As choice is involved with this gift, we must decide whether we create beauty and light or their opposite.

It is a scientific fact that intention influences matter. We all have probably witnessed this in our own lives. When we choose to create, we set into motion a multitude of forces. We draw toward us those in spirit, and on Earth, who seek to assist us. We are inspired by ideas, and we channel the flow of these ideas into reality. We become an expression of the Source when we create for the purpose of uplifting, giving joy, greater understanding, healing, and so on. Our hands become the Source's hands, our minds become the Source's mind, our eyes become the Source's eyes— we become one in the power of creation.

In order to receive creative assistance, we need to first clear our minds of the clutter of everyday life. Go to a quiet place and become still. Once our minds are clear, we can focus our thoughts on that we are seeking to create. Ideas and thoughts will begin to form, and the flow will be started. The clearer our intention is focused, without a multitude of distracting thoughts, the easier it becomes for inspiration to be received.

Action is required in order to create. Once the thinking stage is over, we must take the plunge, plow past our doubts and fears of imperfection, and create. The initial product may be imperfect, and this is okay. We can choose to refine it afterward or even enjoy it more because of its imperfection.

We must avoid comparing our creations to those of others. We are each manifesting individual expressions, and comparisons should only include other pieces of our own creations. Do not envy others for their works. This is a negative energy that will block the flow. Rejoice in the beauty of each other's creations, because this is their purpose. Talents are gifts from the Source and are given to benefit all. By appreciating another's creation, we become partners with the artist. The artist is the hand of God, and through appreciation of the art, we become God's eyes. As we are all one, and our Source is the same, what need is there for envy?

On a personal note:

My best friend, Cathy, had always expressed a desire to paint. She was hesitant and fearful to pick up a paintbrush, however, because she was paralyzed by the fear that she might not be good at it. Years went by, and although she was drawn toward this gift, her fear of failure prevented her from trying. I knew she needed to take the plunge, so I bought her a paint set, and we enrolled in a Bob Ross painting class.

By breaking the ice and picking up that paintbrush, Cathy began to lose her fear of failure. She was so caught up in the act of creation that she forgot to be afraid. Yet even though she had conquered the technical aspect of learning to paint, she felt dissatisfied. She knew her talent and gift extended beyond painting mirror images of another artist's work. She began to experiment on her own and discovered her own style and visions of those images she wanted to create on canvas. Her work is amazing! By pushing past her fear of imperfection, she has created beautiful and haunting paintings.

Creating does not only involve art. It is bringing an inspiration into reality. One autumn, as the weather cooled and the sun dimmed, I was sitting at my computer crying, because in the fall, right on cue, my psoriasis flared up. I'd just called my dermatologist's office and was told it would be about a month before I could get an appointment. Knowing I was getting worse by the minute, this was devastating news. As I sat there crying, I prayed for help. I was inspired to look up the subject online. My search revealed that, for some unknown reason, the Dead Sea helped control psoriasis. The testing of the water only revealed that it was more acidic than other bodies of water. Knowing that psoriasis is an autoimmune disorder (it gets worse every time I get an infection), I concocted my own treatment. In my bathwater, I put aspirin (as an anti-inflammatory), vinegar and a few tea bags (for acidity), and a little salt (the Dead Sea is saturated in salt). Within minutes, I could feel it working to heal my skin. I soaked and scrubbed my skin in this bath each day for a week and was amazed at the difference! The creation of this healing concoction has helped me for years. I passed it on to several other people with psoriasis, and they are amazed at how it helps. (Be sure to check with your doctor if you want to try this!)

Soul play:

+ Take a class in some type of art form that interests you: painting, sculpting, writing, needlepoint, ceramics, playing musical instruments, or composition ... whatever strikes your fancy.
+ Go to an art museum or listen to beautiful music ... become the eyes and ears of God.
+ Decide to plow through fears of inadequacy and the worry that you will create an imperfect product. Concern yourself, instead, with the process of creation.
+ Once the basics are under your belt, utilize the knowledge you gained on these technical aspects. It is time for your own individual expression to be brought into the world.
+ Go to a place you find inspirational. Go alone. Clear your mind and focus on that which you intend to create. Ask the universe for inspiration and listen. Have a pen ready to write down ideas or a pencil to sketch impressions that come to mind.
+ Act! Bring your ideas and art into the world!

Education

Education is the process of seeking and receiving knowledge. There are few things we can take with us when we pass from this life to the next, and education is one of them. This understanding emphasizes the value of learning, and why it is so important to seek the best teachers.

Education is not only obtained in a classroom. Some of life's most important lessons—spiritual and temporal—are learned from life experiences rather than theory or textbooks. Seek to learn from many arenas and all books.

It is said that when the student is ready, the teacher will appear. But be prepared, because these teachers come in a multitude of shapes, colors, and forms. We need to look upon everyone we meet as a potential source of instruction. We must ask ourselves, "Was this person sent to teach me patience? Unconditional love? How to have fun? How to respect myself or another? How to trust? How to forgive? How to change a tire? How to publish a book?" The list is endless! It is only limited by our imagination or lack of desire to learn.

We should seek to acquire knowledge about whatever we have a passion for. This places us in the flow of our life's purpose, much like a tidal current, and learning will be easy and joyful. The attitude with which we pursue a subject greatly affects our ability to learn. When we are enthusiastic, open-minded, and willing to ask questions, this facilitates the process.

The power of three is an important tool to remember. First, we must expose ourselves to the overall view of the subject to be learned. Second, we must seek to understand the subject—immerse ourselves in it, pick apart the pieces, and put them back together again. Third, we must seek to incorporate the knowledge into experience.

It is necessary for the student to understand that there is no failure. There is simply what we learn and what we have yet to learn. "Failure," more accurately understood, is the success of fine-tuning and identifying what we have yet to learn. This is invaluable information!

On a personal note:

While sitting at my kitchen table, attempting a math problem for the fourteenth time, I got so frustrated I wanted to throw my pencil across the room. Why was I doing this anyway? Of what importance would this algebra be in ten years? I thought, *Maybe I should just quit!*

At that moment, my then-nine-year-old daughter Jenny walked into the room and noticed my looming tears of frustration. When she asked what was wrong, I threw my hands up in the air and asked, "What do you do when you've tried to do something over and over and you still just can't get it?" When I asked this question, I wasn't really expecting an answer ... I was just venting. To my surprise, my daughter came over to the table and suggested, in a very mature tone, that I go back to the beginning, reread the instructions, find the part I didn't understand, and try again. I took her advice, this time remembering to pray for some help in understanding and found that I was able to successfully complete the problem. Who would have thought that my nine-year-old daughter would have been able to teach me how to study?

Whenever I come home from work, my dogs fall all over themselves with unrestrained joy over my arrival. It doesn't matter to them if my makeup isn't on and I look like a washed-out blob. It doesn't dim their joy that I scolded them that morning for pulling garbage out all over the floor. Their little tails wag just as much. Who would have thought my dogs would teach me unconditional love?

I have a tendency to go through "spiritual growth spurts," and while they can be painful at first, the results are worth it. Pain is usually the first sign that one of these growth spurts is coming, in fact. I learn a great deal in my search to feel better. When this occurs, I experience humility—and when I am humble, I become teachable.

I know that when the student is ready, the teacher appears, so I pray for someone to come along and help me. Then I have to become conscious of the people I run into. I am often surprised when my teacher turns out to be someone I already know. Once, the teacher turned out to be myself ... in a roundabout way. I was crying in my room, feeling like a failure, and having a private pity party. My daughter Laura sat on the bed next to me and said, "Everything is going to be fine … things happen just the way they're supposed to. What did you learn?" I was floored! I asked her where she learned that advice, and she said, "You!" So we need to be reminded, in times of stress, of even those things we already know.

I keep a library of books that inspire me. When you are seeking to learn any lesson, look for masters in the subject—learn from the best. In my spiritual quest, in addition to the words of Jesus, Buddha, and more traditionally known masters, I gather books by spiritually inspired masters such as Wayne Dyer, Deepak Chopra, Neil Donald Walsch, Iyanla Vanzant, and Sanaya Roman. For help stirring my creative juices, I turn to the wisdom of Julia Cameron. There is a wealth of assistance out there in the world! I've only named a few here. In addition to spiritually helpful books, I feel it is prudent to add that in the effort to be self-reliant, it couldn't hurt to pick up a book on, "What to do when your toilet breaks"!

Soul play:

- What subject do you have a passion for? What are you interested in learning? Go to the bookstore and allow yourself to be drawn toward books that will help you. Are there clubs or groups you can join to learn more? Call up and join! Enroll in a class … you are never too old!

- Pick out a teacher. Choose someone who knows your chosen subject inside and out—a master. Contact this person and express your interest in learning. He or she may either offer you valuable information or direct you on the path.

- Lose yourself in the joy of learning! Open your eyes so you don't miss an unexpected teacher.

- If you "fail" during the learning process, do not beat yourself up! Remember, failure is success in disguise. Evaluate what you have learned, and remember what doesn't work.

- Keep a journal to write down at least one thing each day that you learned. When you re-read this information, it may come at a time when you most need to be reminded!

Efficiency

Efficiency is accomplishing what needs to be done in as little time as possible through focused concentration. It is determining to set aside unrelated interruptions in an effort to complete the task at hand.

In order to have greater balance in our lives, we need to become more efficient in freeing up our time to devote to the enrichment of our spirits, friendships, and families. These are essential aspects of our lives—the most important ones, in fact. Yet, we often have little time left for them after all else is done.

Becoming efficient requires two elements. The first is deciding if the task itself is important enough to bother doing. Is it really necessary to vacuum and dust three times a week? Would once be sufficient? Do you have a possession that requires a lot of maintenance? Do you really need it? Does perfectionism cause you to spend twice the time you should on a task? Would your time be better spent reading a book or throwing a ball to your child?

The second element is to refuse to be sidetracked from focusing on the task. It is so easy to become distracted—the phone rings, there's a knock at the door, the cake looks tempting, we intend to sort through papers but end up reading them, and so on. To become more efficient, we need to send a clear message to ourselves and others that we are not to be interrupted in our focus for a specified period of time.

We must take a few minutes to organize ourselves and gather anything we need to accomplish our task. We need to calculate how long it should take and formulate a plan with timed goals incorporated into it. Time limits will help keep us on track and keep distractions to a minimum.

Our environment must be prepared as well. Answering machines should be turned on, or the phone turned off. A note on the door can say, "Please do not disturb." Make the announcement to everyone that you will be involved with a project and can only be disturbed by those who seek to assist you in its completion.

When you send such a clear message to the universe, you will be assisted in becoming efficient, and others will respect your desire to do so.

On a personal note:

When I want to get something done that I find unpleasant, I have to throw myself into it headfirst. I will procrastinate until the cows come home unless I force myself to just start the project. If I waited to be "in the mood" to get anything done, it just wouldn't get done. But if I start the project, the feeling of accomplishment sets in, and this motivates me to finish.

While self-discipline gets the project started, and the feeling of accomplishment motivates continued action, organization is the key to efficiency. Having a game plan keeps me on track and focused. If interruptions are a fact of life, I keep them to a minimum by letting everyone know what my game plan is. I call in any assistance I can get from everyone around me. After all, if they are busy helping me meet my goal, they are less likely to interrupt me!

Isn't it funny that the house can be a mess and might take all day to clean with perfect standards, but if unexpected company calls and says they will be arriving in an hour, we can move mountains! That's because we set aside our need for perfection and develop an automatic eye for handling the most important things first, without going through each and every piece of paper on the table! That's the kind of mentality that promotes efficiency—getting the most done in the shortest amount of time. Do those papers need to be sorted? Yes. But can you do that later after the house is clean? Yes. Choose your battles. The same is true of any project. Tackle the big stuff first, and focus on the finer points later. I find that when I do this, I get a greater sense of satisfaction because I see results sooner. Otherwise, it is easy to get bogged down in details and feel frustrated.

Whenever possible, do two things at once! If a project requires a phone call to discuss the project, put the phone on speaker (or carry a cordless) while you take care of something else. This will cut down on time.

Make a game of it! If you have kids and they can help with the project, get them involved. Give them something equal to their abilities and set the timer on the stove. Challenge them to have their task complete before the timer goes off. As juvenile as that sounds, it works for adults too!

Soul play:

+ Prepare your environment to avoid interruptions. Turn off the phone, put a note on the door that says 'Do not disturb until – o'clock' and lock it.

+ Decide if anyone can help you to accomplish your goal (or even a small part of it). Consider their skill level, but don't underestimate their ability to be taught. Take the time to show them what you want and how to do it, then let them try. Gently evaluate if you need to be more clear in your teaching if they fail. The time you dedicate to preparing your assistants is well spent!

+ Choose a task that usually takes up a good deal of time—one you find unpleasant and usually welcome distractions from. Consider what you need to accomplish the task. Gather everything you might need so there is no time wasted later. Sit down with a pad and paper. Break the task into parts with smaller goals. List the most important things first. Estimate how much time it will take to finish the task. Challenge yourself to cut the time nearly in half. Then, set your revised time limits. With focused attention, while avoiding perfectionism, run through the actions required to get the job done.

+ Make a game of it—see how far ahead of schedule you can finish your project!

Enthusiasm

Enthusiasm is the joyful expression of passion. It is contagious and fuels motivation to act. In its expression, our own goals become reality and others begin to share our passion. They see in us a joy they wish to share. They are uplifted and energized by the connection to us.

Through the expression of our passion, new insights and ideas will open to us. Enthusiasm is a vehicle through which spiritual assistance can be given. When enthusiastic and thereby enabling a greater inflow of inspiration, our passion is divinely given and ties into our life's mission. Goals, fired by enthusiasm, will bring passion to our life and give it substance.

Do not be afraid to express passion for fear of ridicule. There are too many who stand to benefit to be deterred by the few who may test us. Enthusiasm is meant to be shared. To deny this passion is to dampen our own Light. This can lead to bitterness, disappointment, and frustration.

Passion cannot be half-heartedly expressed. The entire heart and soul must be actively engaged. While in this state, dense or negative energies such as doubt and worry are dwarfed and extinguished.

On a personal note:

When I feel enthusiastic about a subject, I feel electric ... like I am linked into a universal flow of energy and ideas. From this vantage point, it is easy to talk about my passion and get other people fired up about my ideas as well. It is as though my energy sparks out and ignites them.

As is always the case, opposites exist. There are those who say, "It's a great idea, but ..." or "Sounds interesting, but I would do it this way ..." or "That's not practical ...," etc. These people were sent to test our convictions and trust in the power of our passion. They don't usually mean us harm and can sometimes even temper our enthusiasm with some useful information. Take what is helpful and run, don't walk, in the opposite direction! These people, while well meaning, can become toxic to you!

While enthusiasm is meant to be shared, there should be a note of caution. During the process of creation, the flow of inspiration can be a delicate thread, easily cut off by doubt or negativity. While creating, wait to share your enthusiasm about specifics of your project. Wait until you are completely thrilled with what you have accomplished and then share it with full passion. Once the project is complete, the critical words of others cannot be allowed to damage the connection or endanger the completion of your project.

Some people have experienced their enthusiasm being beaten down so often by someone they've trusted that they have forgotten how to tap into this feeling. They may have proudly held up their art project from school to have the most important person in their life glance at it impatiently and comment that they had no time to look, or look for a second and distractedly mumble, "Oh, that's nice, dear." Over time, the disinterest by a loved or trusted one can take its toll on our ability to trust in our own enthusiasm over our creations. We may even have become numb to the feeling.

The way back to finding our enthusiasm in such a case is to understand that you have the ability to regain it—the *responsibility* to regain it! Surely, the thoughtless words spoken by another should not prevent you from the joy of enthusiastically creating for the rest of your life! You need only yourself to nourish this endeavor. Do not share your exploration into enthusiasm until you are totally geared up and sparked up. Forgive those who have unthinkingly dampened your flame, but do not make the mistake of accepting their opinion twice!

Think back to the last time you were electrified by an idea—whether or not someone else cut off the power supply. Why were you stoked by this idea? What did you want to learn or accomplish? Stop worrying what someone else will say and go for it! Immerse yourself in the idea and allow yourself to rejuvenate your ability to feel enthusiastic. Out of the ashes come great things!

Soul play:

+ What do you have a passion for? Don't know? Well, set out to find out! Go to the bookstore and browse the aisles until something sparks your imagination. Ask yourself why the subject was so appealing to you. Is there a way to learn more about it? Can you talk to someone, maybe even the author, about the subject? Chances are, if you were drawn to it, there is a reason.

- Seek out and surround yourself with positive, encouraging people while you are creating an idea. Often, the seeds of your idea will come from some comment, however offhand, the other person might make.

- Look for group meetings that discuss topics that interest you: a book club, a spiritual group, or the Sierra Club (for us nature lovers). Look in the phone book or the library.

- Once you've found something you feel a passion for, think of ways you can create something that can share that passion with others. Bring it into reality; set goals. Nurture your enthusiasm—don't depend upon others for this! Build your enthusiasm (once the project is formed in your mind, the creation is underway) to the point that you are electrified with excitement and ready to spark others.

- Seek out a therapist or doctor if you haven't had the energy to be enthusiastic for a long time, despite wanting to. Chemical imbalances (this can be a sign of depression) can result in this and may need to be treated medically. If you find that you are too tired or drained to even think about enthusiasm, this is a good indicator for the need of medical attention.

Expectancy

———————— ❦ ————————

Expectancy is the pregnant pause before the birth of your beliefs. As in pregnancy, our expectations must be nurtured with positive thoughts, inviting the Source to become the umbilicus. Expectancy is a key element in the manifestation of all things. We must be aware of the need to consciously choose what we expect or our unconscious will do it for us, and this part of our mind—while well intentioned—does not always have the full picture.

A law of the universe states that we attract toward us those things we expect. This cannot be overemphasized because there is great power in this law, and it must be used wisely. As we become aware of our expectations, we can choose to accept them as they are or redirect them in ways that might serve us better.

Negative thoughts result in negative outcomes. Another's negative expectations of our performance or behavior can actually influence us to respond accordingly. This is another reason it is important to be conscious of what we choose to expect, lest our reactions become tied into the negative vibrations of another. When another has expectations that we will be angry, upset, or disturbed by something, we usually are. If they expect us to fail— we usually do. To guard ourselves against such negative expectations, we must be prepared with positive responses and expectations of our own.

There is so much potential in the pregnant pause. Nurture it with visualizations of beauty, love, light, and success. We have the opportunity to focus on our highest visions about how something might unfold. By our positive visions of another, we could possibly even influence them for their good.

On a personal note:

As a child and through high school, I passed my math classes on a wing and a prayer. My teachers commented that I was talented in English but that math and science were just not my subjects. Over time, I came to believe this was true. I accepted the concept that there are certain subjects some people are just not adept at. I began to expect that when I took a math test, I would probably fail or do poorly. And I did. My expectation was that I was just stupid mathematically and there was nothing to be done about it. And since math is essential for science, that eliminated science as well.

When my children were in elementary school, they began to ask math and science questions, and I was forced to tell them that mommy would not be of any help in that department because I was "stupid" in these areas. I began to feel sensitive about my intelligence as a result, and I would take innocent comments from my husband as attempts to "make me feel" like I was inferior. I would become angry and resentful and walked around feeling like a victim. Then I realized I was victimizing myself.

I wanted to go back to school and become a nurse, and I knew that with my current "nonexistent" level of skill with math, I could not get into the program. When I called to inquire about what I needed to do to pursue my dream, I was told that only those with the highest grades in math and science would be considered. Talk about discouraged! I wanted to throw in the towel but had come to understand that all things are possible, and I had to change my expectations of myself when it came to math and science.

I decided I was not stupid and that all I needed to do was to go back to basics and teach myself what my teachers hadn't had the patience or time to teach me years ago. Like a pyramid, I would build my knowledge of math from the ground up. I purchased a basic math book and got to work. I read the book from beginning to end, practiced the lessons, and took the post-tests. I was amazed that I was getting 95–100 percent of the test questions correct! I gained confidence with each chapter, and began to understand that I was not "stupid" in math! And this later translated into mastering my science classes as well.

Had I not changed my expectations of my intelligence, I would not have had the courage to buy that math book, not have gone back to school, and not have subsequently earned my nursing degree. I would not have been hired to make the money to have purchased my home and contribute to the financial well-being of my family. From the small seed of expectancy, all of these wonderful things have manifested in my life, and it can in yours.

Soul play:

+ What negative expectations of yourself or others hold you back or discourage you?
+ Consider a situation where you would like to influence the outcome. Consciously choose to expect the highest, most-positive outcome to this situation.
+ Invite the Source to assist you in magnetizing this outcome and to assist you in changing your expectations into positive ones.
+ Visualize the highest outcome. In your mind's eye, like a movie screen, see yourself or the people in your life behaving and acting positively and lovingly.
+ Maintain the flow of positive thoughts toward your expectation, even if you are tempted to do otherwise! If events or people don't begin immediately to show the effects of the positive expectation, don't become discouraged. It sometimes takes time for the effects to become reality.
+ Observe and give attention to the positive that occurs, and more of the same will follow.
+ Remember to give thanks!

Faith

Faith is the conscious decision to trust in the Source, regardless of outcomes. It is the releasing of fear—that we could be hurt, that something awful may happen, that we might not be able to handle things, and so on. Faith is the throwing open of our arms to the universe and welcoming all experiences with the knowledge that there is nothing to fear.

All of the events in our lives are designed for our soul's growth and the opportunity to express love. We are divinely protected in the fact that regardless of the so-called trials of our lifespan, we will return to the Source from which we come. All is well in this sensing.

Some suppose that in the questioning of their belief system, they are losing faith. This is not so. Many belief systems are based upon the acceptance into ourselves the beliefs of others. It is good to question, for without an openness of mind to "try on," as it were, new beliefs or concepts, we could not grow spiritually.

What we believe today may be very different from what we will believe in a year from now—if we have lived that year with an open mind and heart, listening to and considering new ideas. This does not mean our prior beliefs were "wrong." They were stepping stones. We walked upon them as we cleared our path toward a place where we finally saw the vastness of the universe, and the glorious realization of who we really are in connection with it. We are part of, and contain, the very Source we originate from.

On a personal note:

When I consider how my understanding of truth has evolved over the years, I am grateful that I have been able to open my mind to the possibility that there was more I could learn. Without having had to experience some of the trials in my life, I don't think I would have been able to humble myself to the possibility that my limited view was restricting me.

There was a time that I was inflexible, stubbornly holding on to my organized religion's version of the "only and absolute" truth. I bought the idea that the doctrines and teachings of this religion were the final destination. There is a great deal of relief in this! It meant I didn't have to continue to search and long for truth anymore! I felt special in that I was part of the true religion. So, naturally, I felt duty bound to ensure that every member of my family conformed to the rules and guidelines set forth by the elders in my church.

Imagine my surprise and dismay when my husband and children had their own ideas and their own paths to follow! This didn't fit in nicely with my vision of how things should be. This created conflict and drove a wedge between myself and those I loved. It was when I came to the realization that I was demonstrating a lack of respect by imposing my views upon them that I began to focus more clearly. Respecting their views and right to question helped me to respect my own right to question and explore.

When I am getting ready to grow, I go through a period I call "sacred discontent." During this time, I become deeply dissatisfied with the status quo. Although these periods are not very pleasant, I understand that they are necessary to propel me toward growth. I have learned to open my mind and heart to new information or ideas that will assist me on this path. As I understand now that my greatest learning occurs during these discontented periods, I use them to research and read. I ask for, and receive, inspiration from unexpected places.

Soul play:

+ Make a conscious decision to choose faith over fear. Think of an event you perceive with fear. Place faith upon the situation or event, with the intention that regardless of what happens, you can handle it. How does having faith in yourself change your perspective of the situation?
+ What religious beliefs do you follow? Why? Is there a part of you that is experiencing "sacred discontent"? Ask yourself if you are afraid to question the beliefs you have taken as your own. Remind yourself that it is good to question, and allow your mind to open to new ideas, without unnecessary guilt. Write down your thoughts and feelings in order to see them more clearly.

- Evaluate your responses to the beliefs of others. Are you respecting their right to follow their own path? Are you imposing your judgment of how they should act and which behaviors they should demonstrate? Make the decision to allow them to be responsible for their own path and respect their right to do so.
- Spend some time contemplating that having passed through this lifetime of various trials and imperfections, we are secure in the knowledge that we will return to the glorious Source from which we came. What thoughts or preconditioned beliefs prevent you from accepting such an unconditionally loving return to the Source?

Flexibility

Flexibility is the ability to realign our thoughts and actions to suit the changing circumstances in our lives. It is the understanding that sometimes we must be willing to change our direction in the short run to reach our goal in the long run.

When we have goals in mind, it is easy for us to become narrowly focused on which chain of events should get us to our destination. When something disrupts this chain and life throws us a curve ball, as it often does, it can unbalance us. Here we were, plowing straight toward our goal, when BAM! the unexpected happens and sets us back on our heels. We may be tempted to throw up our hands and give up when this occurs, too frustrated to continue. This is especially true if several curves were sent our way.

When we feel this way, it is because we have a preset course of events in our minds. If we acknowledge that these short-term goals are simply guideposts and stop putting so much emphasis on when we achieve them, we will be less likely to break our commitments. Flexibility is necessary to prevent this from happening. Concentration on the process and being open to alternate routes, without fixating on expectations, allows us the freedom to be flexible.

Sometimes reaching our goals actually requires a five-steps-forward-three-steps-back kind of approach. If we gave up after the two steps back instead of concentrating on the three steps ahead we gained, we would continue to lose ground. Focus on the overall progress, and remember: what we put our attention on is what we draw toward us. Flexibility helps us to remember that the universal Source is in charge of "how and how long."

On a personal note:

I am not always the most flexible of people, especially when it comes to cutting myself a break. So what if I lost twenty pounds? It's the seven I gained back that consumes me, and then before I know it I'm back up to where I started. Why do we do this? I guess its partly human nature, or so many of us wouldn't fall into the same pattern. This is a habit worth trying to break!

Aside from diets, focusing on lost ground applies to everything. We think, "I worked so hard on that proposal, but I could only convince two people on the board." Well, what if we congratulated ourselves on that instead? "So today I convinced two, and after a few revisions, maybe I'll convince a few more tomorrow." If we are not flexible, or won't consider that perhaps our approach needs to be revised, we are throwing in the towel.

Think about it. If the Wright brothers had given up after the first few mishaps, we would still be Earth bound. A few failed space missions and we'd never have had a man on the moon, or satellites that enable us to communicate instantaneously. Who knows the limitless potential of space travel that future inventions will propel us toward? Inventors often need to think "outside the box" and be flexible to find the solution that will ultimately work.

Just like inventors, we need to be flexible with how we approach our goals. If we are prepared to navigate unexpected waters now and again, we can keep our goal afloat. Fate will take us exactly where we are meant to go, even though the process is not always what we had planned. Perhaps the timing is not what we'd expected, or the people we thought we'd be with are not the ones who end up playing an important part. Yet if we stuck ourselves up on the details, we might not get there at all.

Flexibility in our relationships is necessary as well. When friends and loved ones don't always measure up to our expectations, we can usually afford to cut them some slack and give them the chance to recover from their "three steps back." The last thing people need is for us to chime in about how far short they are falling from their goal. I think it's safe to say that they are aware of this and could do with a little pep talk. Which one of us wants our support systems to remind us that we aren't good enough? The best-intended comments can be taken hard, so tread with care.

Soul play:

+ Is there a goal you have been trying to reach, but events keep occurring that are pulling you back? What are these events? Is it possible that they are taking you to your goal in a roundabout way? Are you frustrated with your own progress? Are you ready to give up? Is your frustration due to your refusal to be flexible, either with timing or methods?
+ Decide to focus your attention on the progress you have made and be aware that few goals are achieved without any deviation or backsliding. Don't beat yourself up, but turn the focus toward future achievement.
+ Allow flexibility to give you the freedom to enjoy the process without the pressure, and pat yourself good and hard for any accomplishments along the way.
+ Is there someone you've been reminding that he or she has fallen short of your expectations? Be a little flexible with this person and point out his or her accomplishments. Chances are, he or she needs the support from you.

Forgiveness

Forgiveness is the letting go of anger, hatred, and resentment of another (or of self) that has resulted, in our perspective, from hurtful actions, non-actions, or words. To forgive, we must understand that each of us is at different levels of enlightenment.

To resent another or ourselves while we are yet in darkness or ignorance is akin to being angry with a child for behaving childishly. We, or the other, acted based upon our knowledge and conditioning at the time. In addition to not having been exposed enough to light and love, we (or others) may suffer from an emotional or mental imbalance. We are—none of us—perfect beings. We all make mistakes, have errors in judgment, and sometimes just have unfortunate accidents.

There are more offenses in this world than we can count. Each varies by degree in its ability to elicit pain, based upon the perception of the one feeling hurt. There are those who have a tendency to be quick to take offense due our own conditioning. We need to come to an understanding that we have a choice in the matter. We do not need to have the automatic response to be offended. We can choose to empower ourselves and release our egos.

When we are unforgiving, we continue to pour salt into our wounds. We become an active partner with the one we blame for hurting us, and thereby prevent our own healing. As a result, we resent the one who offended us all the more—not seeing our own part in our pain—and create our own vicious cycle of negativity. This blocks our connection to our Source.

When we forgive, we become free of the harmful spiritual and physical effects of anger and resentment. Stress due to these emotions can result in ulcers, cancers, and all types of physical maladies. The body is sensitive to such negative energy. These emotions cause the spirit to shrivel and shrink, because the positive energy it needs to express itself is drained. With forgiveness, we heal our wounds and raise our own spiritual vibration.

On a personal note:

We all have people in our lives who have hurt us. The circumstances may vary, but the feelings are the same: anger at the unfairness, frustration at the sheer stupidity of that person, hurt that they were so thoughtless, sadness for ourselves for being victimized. Then comes the clincher! "They should *pay* for what they did to me!" The need for revenge creeps up like battery acid into our mind, causing our fists to clench and our throat to close at the very thought of the injustice done to us.

As our stress levels mount, we might start snapping at our loved ones, become distracted and unable to have fun, or stop participating in activities that used to bring us joy. Perhaps we might even indulge in some heavy daydreaming about how to get even and settle the score! This can even temporarily make us feel better, but acting out on it always results in negative consequences. Actions or thoughts that are not a reflection of our higher selves will pull down our energy.

For many years, I was filled with anger at the man who hurt my family. I was the youngest of seven children and don't recall very much, but my brothers and sisters don't have that luxury. Sexual molestation of children was not talked about in the 1960s the way it is today. Schools didn't teach anything about "good" versus "bad" touch, or about what to do when this occurred. Children were to be seen and not heard. Besides, who would believe a child over a trusted adult? What child would have thought to scream, kick, and bite as he was being pulled out of a sound sleep and dragged by his little arm up the attic steps into the bed of this trusted one? How could he have known that his brothers and sisters were suffering the same fate? A small child cannot process such things. But now, years later, as an adult we can certainly process them. The problem is that we carry that hurt child deep within us. The anger we feel now is the adult who wants to protect that child within but finds we cannot or don't know how. Forgiveness is an essential part of the process.

I wanted to know why … for some reason I felt that if I could get into the head of the person who would do such a thing and understand what drove him, it would help me. So I found him and asked him. As is often the case, he had been molested when he was a child. He was profoundly sorry for his actions, as he genuinely loved my family. Although I do see the irony of this, I believed him. We do often hurt those we love.

He found comfort in attributing his actions to being a "stupid kid" at the time, although I would disagree that nineteen years old is a kid! He had long ago come to a place of self-forgiveness, but I was still trying to catch up on the forgiveness part and wanted him to suffer a bit more. He listened while I told him how his actions had affected my family and perhaps even contributed to teenage alcoholism, which propelled my brother into an early death. If I could have blamed my psoriasis on him, I would have. His response was always, "If I could change it all, I would. I am sorry." It seemed too easy! But then I came to realize that he had already done his work at coming to terms with his actions. I was the one who had to learn to forgive.

After I spoke to this man, I realized that my process of forgiveness did not even require that he express sorrow for his actions. Although it helps to understand, sometimes this cannot be the case. A sociopath cannot feel regret for his or her actions. I realized it was *my* process that was at issue. I was the one who needed to put trust in the knowledge that I could choose to let go of the anger and forgive, putting the fairness of life into the hands of a higher power.

Soul play:

+ Consider someone who has caused pain (this can be you or another).
+ Examine the level of exposure to truth and love this person had at the time of his or her actions. Acknowledge the possibility that an emotional or mental illness or imbalance might be present.
+ Make a conscious decision to release your anger toward this person. Send him or her (or yourself) thoughts of healing and peace.
+ Understand that you don't need the other person to feel sorrow for his or her actions in order to forgive. To wait for this person's sorrow is to allow him or her to continue hurting you.
+ Examine what role your ego or preconditioning played in your decision to be offended.
+ Release responsibility for getting justice and give it over to a higher power.

Freedom

Freedom is knowing we have the ability to choose our own thoughts and actions, regardless of the opinions and beliefs of others. In order to experience this freedom, we must release fear of the consequences of daring to think for ourselves. We must risk the displeasure of others who would impose their views upon us.

Freedom of thought is a divine gift to be treasured, valued, and protected. It is the route through which we express our individuality and our right to choose for ourselves. We must not limit this gift by allowing others to decide for us, to choose for us, or to manipulate our thoughts. No one can control our thoughts unless we give that person permission to do so. Ironically, doing so is an expression of our freedom as well. If we have allowed another to set limits upon us, we must recognize that we have given our permission, or we will begin to feel victimized when the other person's will is imposed upon us.

Barriers to freedom of thought are our acceptance of religious, cultural, or societal dictates without consciously evaluating our own opinions regarding whether or not we want to accept them as our own. Often, we create our own limitations based upon the dictates of others. We may have been told by others that following this or that rule makes us a "good" person in the eyes of God. What they may have failed to mention is that our Creator loves and accepts us unconditionally and wants us to feel free to make choices. This is why we are here. Choices, even ones with negative consequences, expand us. They teach us valuable lessons.

Disassociating with outcomes adds to our freedom. When we are not so invested in the outcomes, our thoughts are not bound by pride, fear, manipulation, anger, and so on. Lack of emotional attachment to a specific outcome frees us to respond in whatever manner we choose. We would be wise, however, to consider the consequences as we make our decisions and bring harm to none.

As we learn to cultivate the freedom to think for ourselves, we must remember to give others the same right. When we attempt to dictate to others how they should feel, what they should do, or how they should think, we are attempting to limit their freedom.

On a personal note:

The process of writing this book has been a fascinating one. As I have been inspired to write, I have been given opportunities to learn. The timing of this particular teaching on freedom has also been no coincidence. It seems as though I was meant to wait until this very moment to consider how this topic relates to my life.

Ironically, when I first began to think about freedom in relation to my life, I couldn't identify a single thing in which I had allowed anyone else to determine my own thoughts. After all, I am a free-thinker—and proud of it! So I left this topic to mull in the back of my mind, waiting for the moment when it was ready to bloom.

Last night, while I was lying in bed, accepting that perhaps the mass on my neck was "meant to be" cancer, the answer hit me like a ton of bricks. I was thinking like a good, old-fashioned, Catholic martyr! Someone—most likely a well-meaning priest or nun from my childhood—once taught me that in order to be a saint (or anyone worth listening to about spiritual matters) one had to first *suffer*! Of course, the suffering must be done in silence, and with absolute dignity and stoicism, and the pain must be dedicated to God in order that He might look upon the person with approval.

I remember watching *The Song of Bernadette* as a child, in which Bernadette (a saint if ever one existed), was told by a nun she couldn't possibly be special in God's eyes because she hadn't suffered. In response, Bernadette offered the nun a view of an awful, draining wound on her leg … so awful that the nun began to cry and finally admit that Bernadette was truly a saint. I remember loving Bernadette so much that, in my child's mind, I wanted to be a nun too. I wanted an awful, draining wound to show God how much I loved Him! I wanted to be special in His eyes as well!

So, here I am, years later, with so much more knowledge and truth to work from, and this idea of righteous suffering (which I didn't even realize I still held!) has reared its head! There has been a part of my mind that has been influenced by what the church of my childhood held to be true. I've been writing and discovering truths that transcend the teachings of my childhood ... truths that understand that our Creator does not want us to suffer in order to be close to Him or Her. Our Creator loves each of us and considers us all special. We don't need to suffer to earn this love or to prove ourselves worthy.

What a surprise to discover that part of my mind still held this false belief! I don't need to have cancer to prove to my readers that I can live the principles I write about, and rise above the situation with dignity! I don't have to heal myself in order to prove it can be done! I am amazed at the far-reaching hold the teachings from my childhood have had. On a conscious level, I wouldn't have realized that I still held this belief about suffering, unless my body had manifested this mass on my throat that seemed to scream, "I've had it up to here!"

It would seem the quest for freedom begins with a search for ourselves ... for the nature of our own beliefs, and the discovery of how they originated. We cannot be free-thinkers until we discover the areas in which our thoughts are programmed and begin to question whether or not those thoughts are rooted in truth.

Soul play:

+ If there were no religious, cultural, or societal dictates to consider, what would you do differently in your life?
+ If you would do something differently, why are you accepting the dictates of others rather than recognizing your divine right to freedom of thought and choice?
+ When you hear yourself say, "I should ..." evaluate why you believe this is so. Who is telling you this? Why do you accept their truth or words as your own?
+ When you hear yourself thinking, I should ...—STOP! It is safe to assume you are in the process of limiting your freedom of thought! Discover the root of your thoughts, and hold them up to truth to see if they are still valid to you.

Grace

Grace is the flow of divine assistance. It is a gift from the Source, even when we or others may feel it is underserved. When we can no longer cope or manage on our own, it is grace that carries us through.

We are, each of us, given certain weaknesses in our lives. They are decided upon by ourselves in conjunction with the greater mind of the Creator for the purpose of teaching us to be humble. Weaknesses are also meant to exercise our spirit. Through them, we become stronger.

We must not make the mistake of expecting that, through grace, we can sit back and let this gift carry the load for us. We will be disappointed. The purpose of grace is to assist us when we have done all we can to overcome our weaknesses and find that we are not enough. When we struggle to overcome an addiction, a tendency to gossip, being pessimistic, becoming easily angered, and so on ... we strengthen our spirit.

Consider the example of the butterfly. While in the cocoon, it struggles to free itself, and in the process develops its wings so that it might fly when it works its way out of its confinement. If we open the cocoon to help it along, the butterfly dies. The same is true for us as we struggle to be free of our weaknesses. If grace were to be given to us before we practiced using our wings, we could not grow. We would be denied the experience and strengthening the struggle provides.

The universal law of flow applies with this gift. As with the gift of love, we must become a conduit through which the gift of grace is given as well as received. We have the ability to extend our grace to others as they struggle with their weaknesses. There are times we may look upon someone as undeserving of assistance for some reason or another. It is at these times that we are given the opportunity to practice unconditional love and offer our own gift of grace. Often, God's Grace is given to us by the actions of another. We have the opportunity to become an instrument of His Grace.

On a personal note:

When I quit smoking about twenty-three years ago, I wanted nothing more than a cigarette—after a meal, after my coffee, after a glass of wine—oh, who am I kidding? I wanted them every waking minute, regardless of the occasion. I was smoking up to two packs a day and going strong. I knew I had to quit. I knew it was disgusting to come out of a shower smelling clean and light up, leaving a cloud of smoke around me. I knew I was barbequing my lungs ... sometimes two minutes after having smoked a cigarette, if I pushed the air out of the bottom of my lungs, I could still see a little puff of smoke come out. But as much as I knew how much it was hurting me, I felt I couldn't live without that stick of tobacco in my hand.

When I learned I was pregnant with my first child, it was a catalyst for me. Now it wasn't just my own body I was hurting, so I had to get my act together and just do this. There was no cutting back this time, with some future date as an ultimate goal to totally quit. The realization that, "This is it ... the time is now!" had me in a near panic. How could I do this? I was pregnant and hormonal, preparing for an upcoming wedding (the date of which had to be moved up for obvious reasons), trying to find an apartment, working at my first full-time job in New York City, and countless other stressors. How could I manage without my cigarettes?

The answer was to just do it. It was the *only* answer. I threw my cigarettes in the garbage and prepared for the battle. The end was assured, so that helped. I knew there was no going back for "just one," so I wasn't tortured by indecisiveness. But there were a few times when my car nearly turned, seemingly of its own accord, toward the convenience store to buy a pack. It was during these times that I prayed for grace. I had carried myself as far as I could, but I needed some help over the hills. By accepting this grace, I was able to fight the urge to smoke. When I remembered to ask for grace, my tired resolve was lifted and carried the remainder of the way.

Often our prayers for grace are answered by other people. I remember actually being in line to get milk, aware there were cigarettes behind the cashier desk, waiting for my turn, and fighting the urge to buy a pack. A woman came into the store with her newborn baby. The baby had the sweetest, purest little face, dressed in a white sweater with little pink rosebuds and wrapped with a soft, white blanket. I looked at the innocence and absolute trust and remembered my reasons for throwing away my cigarettes. Had that baby not entered the store at that moment, I may have rationalized (because I'm the queen of rationalization!) that just one cigarette a day wouldn't hurt anyone and would help my sanity. Had the baby's mom not had a sudden urge for the ice cream she came in for, my prayer for grace may have ended differently.

We never know when we are being used to answer a prayer. But if we open our eyes to the struggle of another, we can extend our grace to those who can use a hand getting over their hills and mountains … with words of encouragement and hope, or by actually physically assisting in some way.

Soul play:

+ Consider your weaknesses. Write them down. How have you tried to overcome them? Did it work? Why or why not? How have attempts to overcome them strengthened you? Have they shown you what doesn't work for you? Have they prepared you in some way, as trial runs, for ultimately overcoming your weaknesses?

+ Think of what else might help you strengthen your resolve. Commit to immersing yourself in the struggle. Look ahead for obstacles and strategize how you will solve them. Rise to the challenge! Embrace it with both hands!

+ Do all you can to develop your wings. If you stumble or feel too weak to go on, seek out divine assistance to carry you until you are ready to continue on your own two feet again. Be willing and ready to accept this grace.

+ Look for opportunities to extend your grace to another. You will recognize who needs this by the defeated, helpless look in their eyes. Become God's living instrument of His Grace.

Gratitude

Gratitude is the thankful recognition of the multitude of blessings in our lives. Through its expression, we open the flow to receive.

When we acknowledge the blessings in our lives, we connect quickly to our Source, the origin of all gifts. Gratitude creates an energy that attracts blessings from the universe. It places us in a frame of mind where we are actively seeking out the good in all things and creates joy.

While it is easy to be grateful for the joyful things, we need to be aware of a deeper kind of gratitude. All experiences, even our darkest moments, contain within them many blessings. We need to recognize that these experiences bring the gifts of compassion, growth, and the opportunity to allow others to help us.

There are those of us who cringe at accepting help. We have been conditioned to believe that this is a sign of weakness. We feel awkward and powerless when in need of assistance. We feel we must repay the kindness of others as quickly as possible or refuse it altogether.

We need to understand that there is a time and a season for giving and for receiving. In humbling ourselves and allowing others the gift of giving, we bless those who help us. We have presented an opportunity for them to express love and kindness. Do not worry about "repaying" a debt to this particular person. The universe will bring others in need who will offer us the opportunity to be an expression of the Source.

On a personal note:

It's galling to admit you need help. It's also difficult to accept it. When the kids were little, my husband, Michael, was laid off when his company decentralized their main computer office, and we quickly went through our savings. I remember one day when a friend came over with a bag of groceries for me, and I broke down in tears. She said something that stuck with me—"I am grateful for the chance to help. I've received my share of blessings, and it's a way for me to pass on the favor."

Some of the greatest blessings I've received in my lifetime are the things that have caused me pain. Having psoriasis has made me more compassionate; struggling for money when times were hard gave me a chance to see how generous other people could be; and nearly losing my son gave me a deeper appreciation for the health of my children.... Every event and condition in my life has brought me where I am now, and I am grateful for what they have taught me.

Gratitude can change our whole perspective on life and turn our mood around for the better in a flash. I was sitting on my porch the other day, just after sunrise, feeling inadequate and frustrated. Suddenly, I paused my thoughts and realized I had the choice to feel the way I wanted. I understood that I'd been yearning lately for more: more money, a bigger house, more success, a slimmer body ... and this caused pain. For just a moment, I decided to open my eyes to see the blessings around me. I was sitting on the white porch of the little blue house that God gave me. The sun was dappling the house and lawn and glistening on the raindrops that bubbled under the railings as they plumped up before dropping. We'd had plenty of rain during the season, and I looked out at the grass to see how full and thick the growth was—everything was green and lush. My flowers were bright and colorful on the steps, with fresh new blooms opening.

Inside the house, my family slept—safe and healthy. The breeze lifted my hair gently, and I listened to a symphony of katydids, songbirds, and the pit-pat of raindrops falling from the tree branches to the ferns below the porch. With this attention to the beauty and bounty around me, how could I feel lack? How could I be any richer than this? And from this grateful viewpoint, my day unfolded with happiness and a sense of inner peace— freed from the weight of feeling that my life was somehow inadequate. Realizing that, in fact, my life was full with things to be thankful for.

I've noticed that when other people are grateful for something I've done for them, I am filled with a desire to continue to help them. I have also observed that when I express my gratitude, others want to help me. By expressing and appreciating what we are given in this life, we invite more blessings. If we focus on our lack, we draw that lack toward us. We fulfill our own expectations, and gratitude creates an expectation of abundance.

Soul play:

+ Make a list of all the things you are grateful for. What blessings do you appreciate? Who assisted you in obtaining them? Have you expressed your thankfulness to them?
+ Explore the darker experiences in your life. What lessons did they teach you? How have they enabled you to become more compassionate? Who helped you to get through these experiences? How did helping you bless them?
+ Consider the times you have assisted others during their times of need. How did helping them bring you blessings? How did you feel when you helped them?
+ Think of times you expressed your gratitude. What was the reaction of the people you were thanking? Have people expressed thanks to you? How did this make you feel?

Healing

Healing is the process of replacing something that does not function well with something that does. We may require physical or emotional healing. Through visualization and intent, healing is possible, if it is meant to be. Even illness and death have a purpose in our lives. All challenges are meant to teach ourselves and others important life lessons. Seek the lesson first and then begin to attempt the healing process.

The body has an amazing capacity to regenerate. It wants and works continually to heal itself. The cells in your body reproduce and replace old ones at such a rate that from one year to the next, you are literally not the same physical being you were the year before! What we take into the body directly effects how healthy our new cells will be. Toxins are introduced into our body via choice or circumstance. Some choices we have control over—we are wise to avoid alcohol, harmful drugs, harmful inhalants, stimulants, negative thoughts, and so on.

We have the power to heal our bodies. The mind is an untapped instrument that mankind has barely begun to understand and utilize. Visualization and intent are required. The clearer our vision and intent, the more the brain can work to assist in the healing process. We must actually envision ourselves in a healed state—picture healthy cells overcoming malfunctioning cells.

Be thankful for the experience of the illness—it is an opportunity for growth that offers empathy and appreciation for the health it provides. If we are resentful, angry, and struggling against the illness or pain, we are encouraging its continuance. Let go into the process, give thanks, and then release the illness. Visualize the malfunctioning cells as flowers that were gathered … carry them toward the ocean waves and gratefully lay them in the water and watch as the tide carries them out to sea.

Emotional healing is needed as well. Many walk the earth carrying scars that cannot be seen by the naked eye but can be detected through the lens of love. These wounds can ooze and bleed with fear, hatred, despair, anger, hopelessness, and so on. Some don't even realize the depth of these wounds because they are kept anesthetized by overeating or abusing alcohol, drugs, or other unhealthy coping mechanisms. To assist in the healing of others, visualize them surrounded by healing light and send them love. It will be there for them to assist them if, or when, they are ready.

To heal yourself of emotional pain, go back in time to the experience. Visualize the experience through new eyes—send forgiveness to self or others, surround self and others in the scene with healing light. Thank the experience for the lessons it contained. Visualize the entire scene, in your mind's eye, being lifted by the light higher and higher until it can no longer be seen. Release it with love. Remember—a lesson will repeat itself until it is learned and released with love.

On a personal note:

With pen and pad, I sat meditating on healing and came to the realization that this was one of the lessons I have come to this Earth to work through. I have had a love-hate relationship with my body since I was about six years old, when I began to gain weight. I became disassociated with food as a source of energy and nutrition and turned to it for friendship, entertainment, comfort … you name it. This pattern has remained ingrained in me my entire life.

As an intelligent, successful woman, I find it amazing that I have not been able to restructure my habits to incorporate such a seemingly simple concept as using food for its natural purpose. How have I become so disconnected from my body? Does the answer lie in somehow reconnecting? I promise … when I figure this one out, I will write another book, and hopefully lead other disconnected souls into sanity. None of us were given trials without the seeds to obtain the strength to overcome them. But seeds take time and energy to nurture so they can grow and blossom.

Most of my healing work of late has been centered on dealing with childhood issues of abandonment and betrayal of trust. As children, my brothers and sisters were molested by a trusted family member who lived with us for nine years. I was about four years old when he left. I loved this man with all my heart and soul and looked upon him as a child would a doting father. I was special in his eyes, and this was a treasure for a child with six other siblings. When he left, I was heartbroken. When I remembered what he had done, I was heartbroken all the more.

At first, I covered up my heartbreak with anger. How could someone who had professed to love us do such a thing? I never wanted to see this man again. I hated him for what he had done to my family. It isn't an easy thing to hate someone you love. It creates internal conflict, whether you want it to or not. It leaves scars that rip open when you least expect it.

My healing came when I decided, finally, to contact this man and clean the wound. I told him of my hurt and the hurt he caused my family. I learned that he had been molested as well when he was a child. I listened as he expressed his sorrow for his actions, blaming his history and his youth. I forgave. Not for him, but for me. I realized that unless I forgave, and released the past with love, I could not heal. Even if I had never spoken to this man, I understood that I could complete this process. Even if he wasn't sorry for what he'd done ... I could still forgive and release. The process was within me. I was responsible for my own healing.

Soul play:

+ Consider a situation or experience that causes you pain—physical or emotional. Evaluate what you (or others) have learned or are still learning. What positive results might be associated with it? What have you gained from it? Who have you met because of it?
+ What methods have you used to cope with the pain? Have they helped or caused more pain?
+ Choose an area in which you want healing to occur, and make a commitment to do whatever is necessary to heal.
+ Develop a plan of attack—choose a method, select people to help you, surround yourself with whatever tools you need, and invite the Source to help!
+ Be prepared to forgive ... yourself and others!
+ Envision yourself, and that which you have chosen to heal, surrounded by a white healing light, and open your heart to its energy.

Honesty

Honesty is the ability to accept and speak one's understanding of the truth while remaining open minded that our understanding of it can change. It is the expression, internally and externally, of that which we hold true.

Being honest with oneself, and others, creates a vibration of integrity. Others are not required to accept our truths as their own, or agree with them, or even understand them. It is only necessary that we do, and that we respect ourselves (and others) by not altering our truths to suit another's needs. This does not mean we should be closed to the idea that we might lack a fuller understanding of truth, however. We must be willing to look carefully at our own beliefs to see if a greater light directed at them might illuminate something we hadn't realized before.

Dishonesty is born of shame, fear, and guilt. There is no need for these emotions. We all make mistakes and are often meant to experience them for some purpose. We are where we are right now because of the cumulative thoughts and actions in our lives, and here and now is exactly where we are supposed to be. Sorrow for hurting another is a just and understandable emotion, and this should be honestly expressed. But it should not prevent us from speaking our truths. To be dishonest about our own truths to prevent pain in another diminishes our own integrity and serves the other no true benefit.

On a personal note:

Being honest—true to oneself—is no easy proposition. Sometimes it's one of the hardest things in the world. The only thing that might be harder is reflecting that honesty onto other people when we know their response will be difficult for us to take. Having an understanding that it is okay to be imperfect enables us to speak the truth.

My husband, Michael, and I were going through some rocky times in our marriage. Although some arguments often ended with angry demands, such as, "I want you out of here!," life was just continuing in one endless fight after another. Michael and I can both be hopeless procrastinators, and this situation was just another example of putting off the inevitable. He just could not tolerate the kids as they reached the teenage rebellion years, and this frustration infiltrated the fiber of everyone's relationships. We were all living in misery.

My mother was celebrating her seventieth birthday, and my sisters and I took her to Atlantic City for a show. Afterward, one of my sisters and I stopped for a few glasses of wine. When we saw one of the cast members, I complimented him on the show. My sister went off to try her luck at the slots and this man began to flirt with me. It was disconcerting at first because it had been a long time since anyone had flirted with me, but I was flattered. I felt pretty for the first time in a long time, and I let him kiss me. I stopped it at that, even though I enjoyed it very much.

The experience gnawed at me when I went home, and even though our marriage seemed near its end, I knew I'd made a mistake. I'd taken a situation that was bad to begin with and made it worse. Even though it was only a kiss, I knew it would be the straw that would break the camel's back. I knew Michael wouldn't be able to accept it. But I also knew I wouldn't be able to lie. And my life, my marriage, was feeling like a lie.

A truth, left untold, can save someone from pain, or it can fester and rot away the core of our being. I needed to speak my truth and let the pieces fall where they may. Michael was very hurt, and for that I was truly sorry. I agonized over his pain. I have spent my life trying to soothe everyone around me, and it didn't sit well with me to be the cause of his pain. After all, I was the wife and mother ... up on a pedestal ... how could I have done such a thing?

For a while, I allowed myself to be tortured with guilt. Michael finally moved out. At least now it was my fault, so it was easier for him. But then a very strange thing began to happen. I began to grow spiritually. Out of the ashes of my pain and low self-esteem, I began to bloom. I finally came to understand that although that kiss had been a mistake on one level, it was also a blessing. Without it, my life would have still been in a hopeless limbo ... with everyone miserable. The camel's back needed to be broken so the pieces could finally be repaired.

Don't be afraid, at the very least, to be honest with yourself. People don't always like to hear our truths. We don't always choose to reveal them. Either way, the mirror must reflect a person we love. We are human, and we make mistakes. The first step into self-forgiveness about our mistakes is to be honest with ourselves.

Soul play:

+ Is there something in your life that you have been dishonest about? How has it affected the way you perceive yourself? Are you afraid of consequences?
+ What is the worst thing that could happen if you spoke your truth? Could you live with this? Compared to not speaking your truth … which is more difficult? Living the lie or the status quo?
+ If you feel that speaking your truth would make your life awful, why do you believe this? Could you be making your judgments based on incorrect assumptions? For example, if you have not revealed the fact that you are homosexual, are you denying your family the opportunity to learn unconditional love and acceptance? Perhaps you are underestimating their ability to handle it.
+ If all else fails, and you have decided to bury your truth, you must be able to do so with self love.

Humility

Humility is the understanding that we are all equal spiritually, despite the seemingly inequitable distribution of earthly blessings. There are qualities and attributes that we have been taught to value in this life ... beauty, wealth, intelligence, health, patience, and so on. It is said that we are "blessed" with certain "gifts." Unfortunately, such a belief would have us think there is a God who bestows to some but not to others. This sets up a fertile ground for pride, selfishness, greed, jealousy, and possessiveness to grow. It also precipitates feelings of low self-esteem, sadness, envy, and frustration in the hearts of those who have not been "bestowed" with such gifts. The "have nots" suffer from thoughts such as, "Why is she so blessed while I have so many hardships?"

While it is true that we are each equipped with various so-called "blessings" in this life, the reasons are directly related to our individual missions here on earth. The specifics of these missions are, more often than not, unknown to us. This makes it difficult for us to accept the seeming unfairness of life. Yet, we are equipped with exactly the circumstances we need to complete these missions. Ironically, this might mean that we were "blessed" by illness, poverty, a deformity, a learning disability, or some type of character flaw. Some of our greatest opportunities for growth or teaching come from these "gifts."

Humility comes from the knowledge that, on a spiritual plane, we are all one. We all have access to the same well of wisdom, love, and creativity. If we are all one spirit experiencing separation on this earth, how could we place ourselves above another or feel superior or inferior? This is impossible, as one cannot be better than or less than oneself.

When we understand the true nature of blessings, we see that to value one type of circumstance over another is an error in judgment. We are not special because we have beauty, wealth, or fame; nor are we special because we have an illness or deformity. We are simply experiencing a set of circumstances designed to set the stage for our individual missions. As such, there is no need for jealousy, covetousness, or pride.

On a personal note:

Until somewhat recently, I would look upon others who seemed to "have it all" with a little bit of annoyance, laced with an edge of wanting to steal it from them! There are certain people who seem to just sail through life with grace and ease and look great in that size two dress while gobbling down a third slice of pizza. There are those who can't seem to lose when investing in stocks, obtaining big houses, and buying fast cars. Then, of course, there was that girl in school who read something once and didn't study a thing but pulled straight As while I struggled through each paragraph. It's enough to make us hate people, isn't it?

It is certainly understandable why we might start to think God prefers someone else over us. If we didn't know better, why would we not be envious of that woman who looks flawlessly beautiful without a stitch of makeup? The problem is that we are seeing things as they appear on the outside, without a true understanding of the mission or trials of the other person. Upon closer inspection, we might realize that the very thing we view as a blessing may not be so terrific to live with.

I recently went to a retirement party and was seated at a table with one of the most beautiful women I have ever laid eyes on. She had the kind of face and body that, as a little girl, I dreamed I could have. She seemed very sweet, so I couldn't hate her, even though the thought occurred to me. But it was interesting to watch the other women in the room. They were all nice ladies, warm and welcoming … until they approached the "beauty." I picked up on gossip through the room about how this woman was only promoted because of who she sleeps with and how she looks. I heard about how she might look good, but that she was as dumb as a bag of rocks. Lewd old men made inappropriate sexual comments behind her back. It hit home that perhaps being stunningly beautiful was not such a blessing after all!

As I began to understand the nature of our existence here, however, I could accept that there are reasons for the circumstances we experience. I realized, with a sense of release, that no one is better than I am because they seem to have the things I want. I also realized that some of the things I wanted, in retrospect, would not have been in my best interest. In addition, I began to view some of my hardships as blessings because of the purpose they served in my growth.

It is easier to be humble when you believe you lack what others want. But if fate would have it that we receive such desired circumstances, it is easy to begin to believe that we must somehow be special. This creates a lack of humility and can be more detrimental to spiritual growth than living with less. When we have beauty, we fear old age. When we have money, we fear losing it. In this way, so-called blessings are a double-edged sword. Yet, when we refuse to attach ourselves to the very things that are coveted, we find humility and freedom.

Soul play:

+ What things are you envious of? What people do you perceive of as blessed with these attributes? How do you feel about these people? Can you identify positive and negative qualities about the very things you envy? How can an understanding of individual missions help you to avoid feelings of jealousy?

+ What are you proud of? Why? Do you flaunt your attributes, as if to say, "Look what I have and you don't"? Are you afraid of losing your attributes? How can separating yourself from attachment to these things give you greater humility and freedom?

+ Consider and list your blessings. In what way have they served you? In what way have they hindered you?

+ Be aware of when you begin to feel sorry for another. Determine why. Understand that we don't have a full picture of the soul of the other, or what their mission is on this earth. Understand that the soul is complete and magnificent beyond the earthly experience.

+ Be aware of when you feel inferior or superior to another. Remember at these times that we are all one in connection to Source, experiencing separateness on earth. No one is above or below you. The joy or sadness of one is ultimately the joy or sadness of all. Rejoice for the blessings of others as if they were your own.

Humor

Humor is a state of mood reflective of a particular circumstance or set of circumstances in our lives. This could be connotative of a negative or positive mood, as is true of most things in our world—for opposites are a universal law meant for our learning.

When we are in a "bad humor," we are looking upon situations that occur through this mood state, and the result is, not surprisingly, a further lowering of energy leading to anger, hurtful words, self-pity, and so on. When we are in "good humor," we seek the positive in the situations we are confronted with, resulting in happiness, love for self and others, and so on.

The path to redirecting our humor is by awareness that there is the opportunity to place a situation into an eternal perspective. In the scheme of things, how important is this event or circumstance that has us upset? In ten years, will we look back at this event as pivotal? Based on an eternal perspective, is it possible to find something in the situation that is even laughable? Laughter releases tension, diffuses anger, and invites others involved in the situation to "lighten up" as well. We do not need to take ourselves so seriously all the time.

When tensions rise, or we are embarrassed by an event, look to see if a change in perspective is needed. Be aware of the feelings of others, however, because laughter, if insensitively directed, can hurt someone. Laughter should always be directed from joy and love.

On a personal note:

As I have discovered while writing this book, as I meditate upon a word, something usually happens in my life to give me a better understanding of the meaning or practical application of it. Sometimes, I have discovered, this can be very interesting. When I selected the word humor, I thought,

Oh great, this one may be fun. As it turns out, our perspective makes all the difference.

Have you ever had something really embarrassing happen to you, and although you wanted to crawl under the table at the time, years later you laughed with friends over it? After writing about humor, I was more conscious of trying to look at the lighter side of things in my life and was aware that something might be heading my way to teach me this lesson. I wasn't quite prepared for it when it hit, though.

In an effort to get into some semblance of shape, I had enrolled in a gym with my daughter. Rushing home from work, I called upstairs to hurry my daughter along so we could have time to work out before the gym closed. I noticed my sweat pants lying alongside my gym bag, but was in too much of a hurry to think much of it as I pulled them on and grabbed the car keys.

A half hour later, I was deep into the agony of exercising on a machine in which your legs are sprawled apart and you have to pull them to center and work your inner leg muscles. I noticed a woman across from me working out on her machine and staring at me. As the weight machines all face each other, I did not think this was odd at the time. Then I proceeded to the next torture device, and straddled the padded work bench to do arm presses over my head. I froze in mid press, realizing that I could feel bare leather on my thighs. Cautiously reaching down, my hand encountered the huge hole my dog had apparently chewed out of the crotch of my pants. Do you ever just want to die?

So there I sat, ready to slit my wrists in embarrassment, and my daughter—who must have noticed the scarlet shade of my face and blotches of red on my neck—asked me what was wrong. I explained my predicament, and would have been sadly disappointed had I expected sympathy. As her eyes were tearing from her laughter, I realized I had a choice. I could wait ten years to laugh with her over this moment, or I could see the humor in the situation and enjoy it right then and there. I opted for laughter, and we left the gym in good humor, both thankful that I was wearing underwear!

The lesson here was that I had a choice in my perception and the resulting humor it produced. Had I dwelled on the humiliation rather than the humor, my evening would have been ruined, and I would have missed out on a great laugh.

Soul play:

+ If a situation occurs that embarrasses you or causes you to become agitated, pause and consider it for a moment. Attempt to see the event in an eternal perspective. Envision yourself in ten years looking back at the event. How important was it in the scheme of your life?
+ Invite positive humor into the situation and lighten up your perception of the event.
+ Observe the release of tension you feel and the response of others as you lighten up.
+ Evaluate how the situation might have escalated without your positive humor.

Inspiration

Inspiration is the "breathing in," as it were, of a divine flow of consciousness. We have the ability to receive universal wisdom, as we are part of one universal soul. Whether we are inspired by loved ones who have passed, spirit guides, masters, angels, or teachers, it is all one—all stemming from the Source.

Opening to this inspiration can assist us on our path and make the process much easier. Why should we attempt things on our own when there is so much assistance available, waiting for us to ask? We must, however, learn to ask. We must actively seek to be inspired for it to occur. Ask, in faith, and we receive. We can open to receive guidance in everything imaginable ... writing, art, wisdom, relationships, insight into the hearts and motivations of others ... just name it.

The process of opening ourselves to this universal flow can be as complicated or as simple as we desire. We can engage in meditation, or light a candle to symbolically invite "light"—however we choose to do this is fine, but consistency in our process helps our subconscious mind enter the "flow zone" more easily. Just send out the intention, formulate the questions, and have a pen ready to write.

The ideas may come into your thoughts very quickly—as images, words, or short phrases. They may not be in chronological order. This is because time is an earthly concept and has no real purpose in spirit. While receiving inspiration, our minds are not disconnected to the process. We are responsible for putting all the information we receive into a format that makes sense.

Trust in the messages that are received. Doubt or criticism will halt the flow. It is in the asking, in faith, that we continue to receive.

On a personal note:

This entire book has been a discovery for me in the process of inspiration. I have found that when I have asked the Source for assistance in understanding, wisdom, and clarity while writing about each of the topics in this book, the words and ideas have flowed.

I have chosen to get up early, while the house is quiet, and light a candle with the intention of inviting inspiration with my writing so the words can uplift and assist you, my reader, on your journey in this life. Then, with pen in hand, and my marble notebook on my lap, I focus on a word. Thoughts and ideas come quickly into my mind, and I scribble them all around the word on my page, in no particular order. I formulate questions in my mind and wait for inspiration to answer them.

When I feel I have exhausted all of my questions and have received my fill of inspiration on the subject, I begin to formulate the words and ideas into coherent and meaningful sentences and paragraphs. If I attempted to do this while receiving the inspiration, I think I would have been so preoccupied with the process of writing that the inspiration would have been stilted or lost.

I also noticed that as soon as I doubted that the ideas coming to me were inspired, the flow stopped. I would sit on the couch with pen in hand and have nothing to write. The joy and enjoyment stopped as well. During such times, I had to put my pen down, and go "fill the well" of my spirit. This was done by going out on the porch and watching the birds and feeling the sun on my face, or comforting a patient at work, calling a friend, reading uplifting stories, or anything that made me feel happy. Then, having lifted my spirit, I could reconnect with pen in hand.

We are all connected to the Source, and as such have access to a wealth of inspiration. When we learn to tap into it, we can make our lives so much easier. All we have to do is learn to ask.

Soul play:

+ Set aside time when you are alone and relax your body and mind. Have a pen and pad on your lap. Think of a subject you could use some insight into, or a project you would like some assistance with.

- Formulate a list of questions about the subject or project you have chosen. Write them down, each on a separate page.
- Send out the intention to connect with the divine flow of consciousness and open yourself up to inspiration.
- Ask your questions, one at a time. Write down the thoughts, words, or images that come into your mind. Write all over the page if you want!
- Don't question anything that comes into your mind … there is time for that later. Just write!
- After you have exhausted your questions, reread what you have written and piece it all together.
- Write down in your Soul Play journal what inspiration you have received.
- Remember to give thanks!

Integrity

Integrity is the alignment of one's actions and responses to one's highest beliefs. When one's actions reflect truth and light, the result is a greater connection to Source and to our life's mission. By honoring our feelings and beliefs, we attract people and events into our lives that nourish and uplift our spirits.

Before we can act with integrity, we must first look within to determine what our belief systems are. What are our highest truths about who we are, where we originated from, how we are connected to others, and so on. What higher truths are we learning? Are we afraid to give up beliefs that no longer "fit" as we grow?

Be prepared that when we begin the process of acting from integrity (the honoring of self and the divine within), other people may resist this change in us. This is because they are familiar and comfortable with the old responses and may need time to adjust. Send them love and forgiveness. They will either come to honor us or they will fade from our lives. This is a desirable outcome that opens up space for the soul mates or soul friends who will magnetize toward us.

Do not be afraid of the changes that will occur as we begin to honor ourselves. Letting go of certain people, habits, places, or old beliefs is necessary in the pursuit of integrity. Not honoring self leads to dissatisfaction, frustration, believing others are taking advantage, physical ailments, unhealthy relationships, and so on. Be willing to release whatever it is that prevents you from acting in alignment with your highest truths, and be open to the new and exciting path you will be on.

On a personal note:

Years ago, I joined a religion that brought me comfort and stability and taught me some wonderful truths. It was exactly where I needed to be to learn and expand my spirituality. There were also terrific classes for the kids, and a social bond with caring people for my entire family. Although there were some basic beliefs in the church that I had "difficulty" believing, I probably would have remained content to continue and look no further for truth. After all, the leaders of the church taught us that ours was the "one true church." What was the point in looking further?

As usually happens when we are meant to unwillingly take a spiritual leap, events begin to happen to shake our contentment. The church would have called this Satan's work, but as it turns out, and as I have learned, this is not the case. We are all experiencing promptings toward the next step in our growth, and if we ignore them, *that* is the true shame.

When my husband left the church, it caused a great deal of conflict in our family. I felt personally responsible for his "salvation" and spent a lot of time trying to convince him why he was wrong for leaving. Arguments would ensue because I would push him to accept my views on what he "should" be doing with his spiritual development. It took me a long time and a lot of my own spiritual growing to understand that I was not responsible for his path. It took even longer to understand that I was not honoring his integrity, which had directed him to leave the church.

My own integrity came into question when I looked honestly at my own beliefs in comparison with those of the church. Although I had learned a great deal from many wonderful people of this church, I felt that there was so much more to learn. I felt a sacred discontent. And I felt guilty for feeling this way. But there was an inner voice that honestly acknowledged disagreement with certain teachings of the church. There was an inner voice that did not believe in the right of a separate organization to make declarations of how I should dress, what I should eat or drink, what I should believe as truth, and so on. I was thirsty for spiritual growth, and I felt confined within the boundaries of church doctrine.

It took a great deal of courage to look outside my spiritual comfort zone. There were many who, out of a genuine love for me, tried to tell me I was wrong to leave the church. I will always love them, but they have come to understand that I must follow my own path. Some of them have faded from my life while others remain good friends. Who knows? Someday my path may even lead me back to that church … which is fine, if I have reached a place where I accept all of their beliefs as truth. But for now, as a result of my courage to honor my own integrity, I have learned amazing truths, expanded my view, and have limitless opportunities to continue my spiritual growth. My path has become exciting in its very uncertainty.

Soul play:

+ Behave in alignment with your true desires and feelings, honoring yourself and the divine spirit within.
+ Observe the responses of those around you. Do not allow another's response to sway you from your integrity by manipulation (e.g., anger, attempts to make you feel guilty or wrong, bribery, threats, and so on).
+ Watch for the arrival of new people (possibly even ones you already know) who will begin playing a greater role in your life.
+ Become aware of how these new nurturing, positive relationships enrich you.
+ Review your own actions: are you guilty of not honoring the integrity of another?

Joy

Pure joy is the experience of communion with our Source. It is an experience that, once felt, is not easily forgotten. It is the opening of our hearts to our Source's unconditional love and allowing it to pour through to us. It can cause our hearts to swell, our skin to tingle, and our eyes to fill with tears of gratitude at the wonder of it.

Stirrings of joy are rooted in our ability to appreciate the abundance in our world. Nature is a great arena to stir joy. Listening to the rhythm of ocean waves, feeling sweet, warm sunlight upon our face, the wind lifting our hair, standing on a mountain overlooking a glorious expanse of earth and sky … all of nature's wonders stir appreciation.

Another way to feel joy is to be in the presence of creation or to be involved in the act of it. Standing before great works of art, reading poignant poetry, writing a story, building a chair, watching the birth of your baby, or hearing her laughter bubble up for the first time—all of these stir joy.

There are many who do not experience the pure joy of communion because they feel unworthy to receive it. No one lives a perfect life, and we have all done or said things we may regret. This is expected! We are here to be imperfect—to experience making mistakes and dealing with the consequences. But make no mistake about this … the joyful communion of spirit with our Source is available to all of us whenever we seek the experience with a pure, self-forgiving, appreciative, and loving heart. It is within our power, always, to open the door.

On a personal note:

Isn't it funny how, when you were very young, you used to believe what "authority" told you, without question? And isn't it a blessing that we learn to think for ourselves? When I was growing up, I loved to get dressed up and go to church. In the beginning, my parents came with me. But at some point as I got older, I guess they decided they had done their duty and left me to my own devices. I got lazy sometimes and began to skip some of my Sunday morning visits, but the priests told me that if I'd skipped the week before, I wasn't "worthy" to receive communion. I believed them! And this feeling of unworthiness caused me to feel further distanced from God.

Never let anyone tell you you're not worthy to receive communion with your Source! Most of all, never tell yourself this is true! Your connection is unquestionable. Your entitlement and access to this connection is always available to you. It is actually when we feel the least worthy that we need to understand this the most. The loving energy of our Source is unconditional. We are the ones who put conditions on our love. We are the ones who decide that we are unworthy, and it isn't necessary. In fact, it's detrimental.

The first time I felt what I assume people refer to as "the spirit," I hadn't been to church in years. Not even the Christmas or Easter obligatory visit. I was turned off religion in general and felt disillusioned by it. It felt like there was this hole inside ... an important part of my life was missing. When I realized it was a spiritual hole, a spiritual yearning to be part of something more connected somehow, I decided to try something I hadn't in a long time. I prayed. Not the standard, prewritten, memorized variety. I talked to God as if a friend who knew my heart and soul were in the room with me. I expressed my emptiness, my yearning to be reconnected with spirit. I explained my disillusionment with religion, and desire to learn more about spiritual things. I asked for guidance to find inner peace and satisfaction. Then I offered my thanks for the blessings in my life. As I expressed my appreciation and gratitude, something happened that I'd never experienced before. My body began to tingle, and the hairs on my arms stood on end, and the area around my heart felt so full and warm it might burst. As this sensation rose to lift the roots of the hair on my head, I was so filled with a loving presence that my eyes filled with tears. And I knew beyond a shadow of a doubt that I was in communion with energy beyond anything I'd ever known—the Source. I felt pure joy. And the wonder of it filled me with gratitude.

I was so excited by this experience that I ran out to tell my husband about it. He looked at me as though I was perhaps losing my mind but didn't comment too much about it. I began my spiritual quest and contacted people from a multitude of religions. I was so excited when I discovered I was not the only one to experience these phenomena of spiritual connection to the Source! I wasn't imagining it! And even better still, it doesn't matter what religion you're affiliated with! This connection is available to all of us.

Soul play:

+ Take some time to lie on your bed when the house is quiet. Let your mind and body relax. If you think you might fall asleep, use a comfy chair instead.
+ Send out your intention to connect to your Source. Don't wait to feel connected … just know you already are.
+ Express your innermost yearnings … talk about why you are seeking to reconnect with your spirit. Don't use pre-scripted prayers … speak from your own heart. Know that nothing you can say will cause the presence of the Source to love you less. Bare your heart.
+ Offer the gift of appreciation for all of the things and people in your life that you are thankful for. Don't make it a thoughtless listing … dwell upon why you are thankful for them.
+ Finally, sit quietly for a few moments … focus only on the peace and loving awareness of the connection. Allow yourself to open up to answers or direction. These will come in the form of your own thoughts.

Light

───────────── 🌳 ─────────────

Light is a radiation of energy that contains love and truth. It originates with the Source. Many call the Source by various names—God, Allah, Jehovah, Lord, and so on. It is all one and the same Source.

This radiation of energy is always seeking to enter places of darkness but cannot do so without our permission. There are those of us who cling to places of darkness within our own hearts, preventing light from healing us.

Allowing light to enter our darker thoughts requires forgiveness and opening our hearts to the possibility that we can choose to fill ourselves instead with love and healing. While surrounded by darkness, it is easy to believe there is no light. We must open our eyes and look for it! We will see glimmers of it in other people, or in books, or in art … the very act of seeking it will bring the light toward us.

In the beginning, when we open to light, we may fear being blinded by how much is available and mistrust it. We do not need to fear this because we are in control, and we can decide how much truth and love we are ready to accept. We are in charge of deciding to forgive ourselves and others and to allow healing to occur. Some of us open all at once and embrace the light. Others are more cautious and less trusting that something so good can be real. Perhaps the scars of experience are deep. But light can penetrate the thickest areas—if we want it to. We all learn and receive at our own pace, and this is fine.

As we seek the light, we need to be prepared to open our minds beyond religious boundaries, as truth and love are found in all religions. If we expose and open ourselves to all religions, we can learn something from all of them. We can choose to hold our beliefs, and the beliefs imposed upon us by others, up to the light of love to determine if these beliefs still ring true. Any belief that advocates harm to others comes from darkness, not from light.

There are areas of the world as well where darkness predominates. When in these places, we must be very conscious of connecting with the light of the Source. Darkness can threaten to influence us and dim our light. In these times and places of darkness, we must remember that we *are* the light and can shine as a beacon of hope to others looking for a way out. By responding to darkness with forgiveness and love, the light shines for others to see.

When we share our light, we must be sensitive to the receptiveness of others, so they do not fear opening their eyes. When we act as teachers, the awareness of the readiness of the student is a key factor. We have to be careful not to blind our students with too much information, or they may close their eyes with disbelief.

On a personal note:

I hear the news and feel so sad at the lack of love and forgiveness that permeates the Middle East. There are scars that go back generations on both sides of every issue. These scars are carefully reopened and salt poured into them in order to keep them fresh. Parents teach their children the skill of hatred and revenge in order to keep the tradition of war alive. They do not do this believing it is incorrect thinking ... they feel completely justified and responsible for teaching this, because they have accepted the belief that this is their reality and truth. This teaching causes further acts borne of ignorance and darkness, which perpetuate the need for continued revenge.

At some point, a generation will have to open themselves to a new wave of thinking and realize that the old tradition of hatred is outdated and self-defeating to themselves and their children. With the help of technology, more and more young people are exposed to computers and have access to hearing other voices with more reasonable messages. These children will have the chance to learn that there are choices in this world that can lead to a happier existence. I believe that, over time, as more people in this world have the chance to be exposed to another way of life, they will begin to seek out joy instead of revenge.

Darkness is simply something waiting for light to enter. I believe the parts of the world that live in darkness are beginning to see glimmers of light entering their reality, and once they grasp onto it ... the darkness will recede. There will probably always be corners or pockets of darkness and hatred on Earth—but as the light of truth, love, and forgiveness become the predominant culture, we have a greater chance to coax the darkness from the shadows and into the light.

Creating this culture of light begins with us. Individually, we are powerful, but when light is combined, we perpetuate the new wave of thinking that will ultimately change the world. In our own lives, we can choose to love instead of hate, forgive instead of hold a grudge, and seek joy instead of harbor resentment. In our communities, we can perform acts of kindness and set an example. We can express light in all of our creations so others will see and be drawn to it.

Soul play:

+ Set aside religious boundaries and explore the teachings of Buddha, Mohammad, Jesus Christ, the Kabala, the Torah, and so on. Spend the day at the library and immerse yourself in the adventure of freeing your own mind.

+ Write down insights or inspiring words. Make a study of which core beliefs are similar to each religion. Don't get bogged down by the study of rituals ... this isn't important in this soul play. We are looking for words that reflect light and love ... words that uplift your spirit and ring with truth.

+ When watching the news, instead of condemning those who perform acts of darkness, consider the conditioning they have had their entire lives, and forgive. Send them prayers that they may open themselves to a new wave of thought. Visualize light surrounding them.

+ Make a list of acts of kindness you might perform in your home or community which will be a beacon of light for others to emulate. Set out to do at least one thing a week on your list. If possible, try for daily, because as we share our light, our own shines brighter.

Love

Love is the purest of vibrations ... it is the living energy of the Source. This energy has no boundaries ... it is eternal and infinite. It lives within each of us, connecting us to our Source. We each choose to what degree we open ourselves to this vibration. The connection is unconditional. Our perceptions, however, can limit the flow.

We have the power to change our limited perceptions and open ourselves to become a conduit for this pure energy. It is through the process of giving love back to the universe that we open to a greater flow inward. As a river must receive the flow of water and empty itself into the sea, we also must be as a river with our love. When we freely give that which we seek, we will receive in abundance.

Conditional love is not love in its purest vibration. When we believe that we or others are unworthy to receive this gift, we place conditions upon it and block love's flow. The Source places no such limits or conditions upon us.... Love is unconditional and infinite. When we understand and accept this truth, we can come as we are, with all our imperfections, and open ourselves to this healing and uplifting gift.

On a personal note:

The times I felt unworthy of love were, without a doubt, the times I needed to feel its warmth and security the most. Love is all around us in so many forms ... the smile of a passerby, the driver who waves us to go first, in the eyes of a friend, in the wagging tail of a dog. But unless we open our eyes and look to find it, we don't realize the abundance is right in front of us.

I can get so caught up in worrying about how much love is (or isn't) being expressed to me that it's easy to forget that I should be equally concerned with how I am expressing love to others. In moments of clarity and selflessness, when I focus on how to demonstrate my love, I have found its warmth surround and fill me as well.

Sometimes, loving takes courage. I remember a time when I was uncomfortable even saying the words "I love you." As a child, my family was not free with this expression. As a teenager, I was moved by the urging of the great teacher Leo Buscaglia on the subject of love. Leo was so passionate about the topic that the media named him 'The Love Doctor'. I don't think the man passed a single person on the street without hugging them. His demonstratively effervescent example was contagious. He challenged everyone to open up and express their love. So I committed to giving it a try. I decided that the more often I said I love you, the quicker everyone would be more comfortable with it. At first, the words were practically forced through my lips, and I cringed a little, wondering what reaction my family might have. At first there were facial expressions of surprise and then an equally uncomfortable response of "I love you too." Before long though, it became a natural and enjoyable expression of caring.

Some people are intimidating to love. They can be hard and gruff and outwardly appear as if love is the last thing they are looking for. Don't be fooled ... these are the ones who need our expression of love the most. Their hearts have likely been bruised and need healing.

When I came to the realization that love is not something outside of myself that needs to be sought and found, I gained such a sense of gratitude and relief. I don't need to seek out what I have. I *am* love ... and so are you!

Soul play:

+ Examine your beliefs about who you feel is not deserving of love (including yourself) in your life. What has this person done to be unworthy in your eyes? Visualize this person at his or her purest soul level, with the understanding that this person's actions are side-issues. Envision a golden light surrounding this person's heart, filling him or her with warmth and comfort ... send this person a flow of unconditional love.

+ Consider ways you can demonstrate love to those around you, and practice expressing it. If you are uncomfortable saying "I love you," practice it until it comes naturally and easily. Watch for the reactions of those you say it to.

- Choose someone you know who is cranky and irritable. Make a conscious effort to seek this person out and perform acts of kindness for him or her. Determine that you will overlook any initial suspicion on his or her part and continue to demonstrate caring . I dare you to take it a step further and hug this cantankerous person! It could be that you are giving that person the first hug they've had in years! Every human being needs a good hug—some of them have just forgotten how it feels and need a reminder. Observe his or her response as he or she begins to accept your kindness.
- How will focusing on the truth that love is not something you need to seek outside yourself help you gain inner peace?

Loyalty

Loyalty is acting firmly and consistently toward our values. Loyalty to self is the truest form of loyalty. Loyalty to others is a loving gift but is considered wise only when such devotion does not oppose our own values.

When our actions are not in concert with our values, and we have set aside our own beliefs in order to appease another's sense of what he or she believes the right thing to do is, we are displaying misplaced loyalty. When this occurs, we need to examine whether this loyalty brings us joy or discontent. If it is the latter, we must reexamine our motivation, and we must decide whether future loyalty to something that brings us misery is worthwhile.

In examining such misplaced loyalty, let us try to determine where this value stemmed from. Did others teach us their beliefs and encourage us to accept them as our own? What benefit does this value serve us? Do we believe there are negative consequences to releasing this value? Why? Who told us so? What was their motivation? We are presented with countless opportunities to be loyal to others—parents, spouses, children, friends, employers, and country—this list is expansive. Displaying loyalty to these loved ones and others is a noble trait, but it is only positive as long as our own values are our first consideration. To be loyal to another at the loss of following our own hearts is not true loyalty. It is, in fact, blindly disloyal to self.

On a personal note:

My husband, Michael, and I recently went to Newport, Rhode Island, for a romantic getaway. We stayed at a lovely bed and breakfast called The Cliffside Inn. The history of the inn was intriguing.

The inn's former owner, Beatrice Turner, had a tragic life. She was a beautiful and talented young woman who went away to school to study painting. She discovered her passion for art and was happy to experience a small level of freedom while away from home. But when her parents found out that the school was allowing its students to draw the naked human form, they pulled her from her joy and forced Beatrice to give up her passion. As this was devastating to their only child, they agreed to allow her to paint self portraits.

Her parents, particularly her father, would not permit her to date the eligible young men who came to call and encouraged her to believe most suitors were beneath her. She remained loyal to her father and did not date, and the years passed. Her father died, but instead of using the occasion to mark the beginning of freedom, she felt the need to take care of her mother and assist with the financial and practical running of the household. More years passed, and when Beatrice dared to express her discontent with her spinster life, her mother told her she had no one to blame but herself.

Beatrice became a local outcast, and children would be frightened to pass by her lovely house near the cliff. The adults would gossip about seeing her on the cliff walk dressed in Victorian garb years after it was no longer fashionable.

When Beatrice died, leaving no heirs, the solicitor entered the estate to find it had been painted entirely black inside and was filled to capacity with painting after painting of self portraits of Beatrice in her youth. Thousands of these masterpieces were gathered and thrown together to make a bonfire to protest the sin of such obsession with oneself. Someone saw their value and managed to save a few hundred, but most of Beatrice's life work went up in flames. Her paintings are in each of the rooms at the inn, and I was struck by the unfairness and tragedy of such a life.

I was also struck by the fact that her mother was right—it was Beatrice's own fault that she lived an unfulfilled life. She had placed the values of her parents above her own needs. The values of her parents … even though they resulted in personal misery for Beatrice … were given a higher importance than her own passion for life and her art. What a tragic example of not placing enough importance on the value of loyalty to one's own happiness and joy!

Every day, in some way, we have opportunities to decide to be true to ourselves or not. Every time we may say yes when we would rather say no, every time we may laugh at a joke our heart knows is offensive, every time we may lie rather than deal with consequences, every time we may look the other way rather than confront reality ... these are the moments we may choose to express loyalty to ourselves. These are the moments in which choices are made that define who we are.

Soul play:

+ Think of a situation where you were given an opportunity to be loyal to your own values. How did you handle the situation? If you were disloyal to self in order to please another, how did you feel afterward? If you felt bad, did you continue to remain disloyal to your own feelings? Examine why you placed another's values above your own. Write down your insights in your journal. These will be valuable to reflect upon in the future if similar situations arise.

+ In situations when you were not loyal to your own values, did you feel diminished in some way? Reflect upon the consequences of this disloyalty to self. Do not beat yourself up over what you perceive to be mistakes. All of life is a learning experience, and each event it contains is worthwhile. Write down all your thoughts about the consequences of your actions or inactions.

+ How can developing a clearer understanding of your own values help you to be loyal to yourself? When defining your values, consider your highest vision of who you want to be.

+ If you are accepting another person's values as your own and this is causing you pain, examine whether it is necessary to continue to accept this experience into your life.

Obedience

Obedience is the alignment of our thoughts and actions to the law of cause and effect. This refers not to the rules of men but to universal law.

To most of us, even the word obedience causes us to feel frustrated and claustrophobic, ready to run in the opposite direction. Obedience requires putting aside our ego, which balks at being "told" what to do, and giving our will over to the greater will of the Source.

To do this, it helps us to remember that our free will is supreme. We are always free to choose our thoughts and actions. To do this wisely and to avoid pain and discord in our lives, we would do well to consider the physical and spiritual laws of cause and effect.

The truth is that obedience to physical and spiritual laws does not restrict us as much as it frees us to a greater extent to enjoy our lives. When we choose not to allow toxins into our bodies, we experience greater health. When we choose to exercise the body, we enjoy strength and freedom of movement. When we choose a course of action that brings happiness and love toward another, we experience joy.

It is essential that we become aware of opportunities to be obedient to these laws and to understand their purpose. Their purpose is to teach us how to make wise choices and develop self-control. We are presented with these opportunities on a continual basis. We frequently refer to them as temptations. They offer us the chance to discover the laws of cause and effect and to exercise our self-control.

We can choose to learn these lessons on our own (which can be time consuming and result in personal pain), or we can learn from the experiences of others. It is up to each individual to choose. We are given the creative tool of visualization and imagination and can use them to discover what the effects of certain thoughts or actions would be. If we remain unsure of the wisest course of action, we can consider that the most loving option would be best and ask for inspiration in making the right choice.

Becoming aware of opportunities to think or act in a way that result in positive energy is the key to recognizing how obedience to natural law brings us ultimate peace. Through conscious awareness, our choices may be more directed to this end.

On a personal note:

Obedience and I don't always get along very well. I'm one of those people I was referring to when I said some people balk at being told what to do. I prefer to be the one who sets the rules. When I was involved in various churches, it seemed to me that "obedience" to church doctrine was being pushed upon me, and I balked. I didn't want some outside organization telling me what to do.

When I consider natural law, things make much more sense. Cause and effect—it's as simple as that! If I choose this, that is the result. I decide ... and I live with my consequences. Making wise choices is the same as being obedient to natural law. This is something I can work with! It isn't someone else telling me what I should do.

For example, I know from past experience that when I drink too much caffeine, my heart races and I get irritable. I am more prone to yell at my children and my husband and would be more likely to say something hurtful because of my irritability. I also know that the caffeine makes me feel more awake and interested in getting things done quickly. So I have to weigh my options. Is the potential for taxing my heart and doing something unloving worth the small jumpstart I get from the caffeine? If the answer is yes, am I dealing with an addiction? Can I minimize the consequences by only having one cup? Can I do something healthier to get that rush of energy? The choices we have are limitless.

If I decide to watch a great TV program instead of tackle my project for work, I need to be conscious of the consequences and visualize them in my mind's eye. I am the world's worst procrastinator at heart, and if I am not aware of consequences, things will pile up. So I have to school myself to make conscious decisions and not live without thought to consequences. Inaction itself is a choice, and we often don't realize this.

Soul play:

- Become aware of the opportunities in your day to be obedient to the law of cause and effect. What effect would you like to create? How will exercising self-control assist you in creating this effect?

- Consider an opposite scenario ... what would you prefer to avoid as a consequence? What actions or thoughts might bring about the unwanted results? How can choosing not to exercise self-control lead to this consequence?

- Make a decision to be completely conscious of "temptations" in your day. Consider them opportunities and avoid being resentful of their appearance. Can this change in perspective energize you to look upon self-control as something more positive?

- Write these temptations down as they appear, and list possible consequences or various courses of action you could take. Which is the wisest choice? If you still don't want to choose the wisest course, why? Is addiction involved? Can you minimize the consequences by moderation or a third choice? Write down any consequences that occur.

Oneness

We are all part of one soul, fragmented in order to experience separation, yet joined by our connection to Source. It is through the separation that we appreciate the rejoining and return to Source. How can we truly appreciate our connection without first having experienced its opposite?

It is for us to understand that the separation is only a paradigm. No matter how scattered or far apart human beings are (due to religion, race, age, politics, etc.), we are all joined by the thread of the divine that lives within each of us.

There is much power when we join with each other in unconditional love. As the flame of a single candle lights a darkened room, the addition of another candle increases this light. In this sensing, earth is the darkened room, and we are the candles. The light (love) we carry must be shared with all, especially with those whose flame has been dimmed by hurtful life experiences and those who are "difficult" to love.

When we bring hurt to another, we are, in effect, injuring ourselves, diminishing our own flame. There is a ripple effect to every act ... every thought ... and we all swim in the same lake, as it were. Every act or thought intended to send out love increases our light and illuminates the world a little brighter. If enough of us focus on this intention, it is not impossible to experience peace on earth.

On a personal note:

Do you ever have people enter your life you just couldn't stand? Their views are so opposite your own that you just can't get along? Or they are just so miserable that you can't stand being around them? How can we possibly be one soul separated at birth? The thought is enough to make us cringe!

Cringe though we might, we *are* one. We are here to experience separate existences, and to follow separate paths, but we all share the divine thread. Some of us don't recognize this divine presence within us and are strongly influenced by the negativity in the world. Some don't understand that every thought and action not based on love creates darkness. There are those of us who are so caught up in the energy of revenge or being "right" that they perceive their acts of violence as justified or good.

What they don't perceive is that their actions create more violence and the need for revenge from those they have victimized, and the ripples go forward. Before long, more and more people are involved and the darkness multiplies. Energy, of any kind, is contagious.

There are times (usually when I'm riding out a wave of hormones) that I vibrate with negative energy. No matter how I try, my thoughts wander back to irritation and to looking for what's wrong with the people around me. This is usually when I practice my positive thinking muscles the hardest. I can actually feel the negative energy spread out from me, and soon my husband and children are snapping and quarreling ... the ripple effect in action.

By firmly changing the direction of my thoughts and actively seeking out what in my life I am thankful for, I can usually turn the tides of negativity in my home. A word of thanks, a smile or gesture of appreciation or love, and everyone's mood improves ... the ripple effect.

If this can be accomplished in a home, by one person, why can't it also be true of the world? It takes the power of one, multiplied, to make a difference. Each individual counts. It *is* possible to send out love and good thoughts to each other and have others respond to it.

When I have focused on the connection and the divine spark in another person, the differences in the other have faded into insignificance. My love has had an opportunity to demonstrate its power and has created sisterhood and brotherhood in this realm as well as on the soul level. This is our greatest challenge here on Earth.

Soul play:

+ When are you at your least loving?
+ Who do you feel least connected with?
+ How can viewing these people as extensions of yourself, pursuing an alternate path, change your view?

- The next time you interact with someone and find yourself looking at all the differences between you, acknowledge the same thread of the divine that runs through you both, connecting you.
- How does acknowledging a connection at the soul level enable you to act and feel different about the other person?
- Send out positive ripples and notice the response of others to it.
- If all else fails (because we are human beings with faults), and you do end up sending out negative energy, allow yourself to view the lesson of how negative ripples create more darkness.

Openness

Openness is a state of mind and heart in which we acknowledge that we are continually learning and expanding upon our current level of wisdom. It is knowing that we can find this wisdom in unexpected sources.

If we assume we already know it all, or become so attached to our belief systems that we will not expose ourselves to other ideas or perceptions, we are setting limitations on our own growth. By closing our minds to other possibilities, we create cages we must live in. Once we have decided there is nothing more to learn, we learn nothing.

Belief systems can be restrictive if we consider them to be the final answer. They need to function as stepping stones to greater revelation. Once we believe we have the final answer, we cease asking questions. We must not be afraid of proving ourselves "wrong." We are neither wrong nor right in our beliefs. They simply are what they are and serve their purpose while we hold them. They usually direct us toward greater truth.

To become open–minded, we must expose ourselves to ideas and beliefs that are not our own. Often when we have found a baseline set of beliefs we are comfortable with, we seek only to surround ourselves with people, books, and thoughts that support this view. This is fine for a time. But to open our minds for greater revelation of truth, we must seek to expand our comfort zone.

We must seek instead to surround ourselves with beliefs and perceptions that differ from our own. We must be willing to take a new idea and sit with it for a time. We must be able to view this new idea as potentially holding wisdom. Then we can turn it over in our minds and explore it. We must set aside preconceptions and be willing to "try it on" for a bit to see how it feels. Does this new idea bring forgiveness, peace, love, and joy? Use this question as a compass, as this is the best indicator of truth.

On a personal note:

I like to think I have all the answers, and more often than not this kind of attitude closes my mind to limitless possibilities. Before you know it, years can go by and you find yourself feeling a void ... as though you have collapsed within your own mind and heart. Then, after you feel as dried up of enthusiasm as you can get, you realize that in order to become like a child again, you have to remember to question life the way a two-year–old does and endlessly ask "Why?" and "Why not?"

When we are open to new possibilities and paradigms, we become childlike again, and our enthusiasm knows no bounds other than what we restrict ourselves with. When we find ourselves deliberately excluding an idea as a possibility, we need to look closely and ask ourselves "Why?" Why is the idea something I don't want to consider? Why don't I want to learn about or "try on" this idea? What have I been taught that prevents me from being open to this concept? Who taught me to resist new ways of thinking? What were they afraid of?

I remember driving home from work, listening to a book on tape titled *Conversations with God* by Neale Donald Walsch, which presents the idea that every condition humanity experiences has been chosen by us, either collectively or individually. Now, I'd agreed with the concept that we planned, in large part, the afflictions we would experience in our lifetime. But earthquakes? Tornados? How could I have been part of that decision? Maybe I'd chosen to have psoriasis for some soul purpose ... but how was I responsible for some tsunami in Thailand? My first reaction was to blow off the idea because it didn't fit with my current beliefs. But I decided to open my mind and try the idea on for a few days and mull it over, with the understanding that it was possible that this might have some merit.

The more I thought it through, the more sense it began to make. I already believed that all of us are joined with the Source, and as such are connected to each other. We are all parts of the great whole. So, collectively, it would make sense that we'd planned conditions and events on earth to further give us opportunities to express our love for each other. Without adversity, we would be living in an innocent paradise, and that is not our purpose here. It is through the difficult times that we have the most opportunities to reflect the God Source within us. The hard part is for all of us to understand that we are all responsible for responding to the world's crises and calls for help.

Its so easy for us to get caught up in our own little dramas and drive for more and better things, and to lose sight of lending a hand to someone in need—especially when that person is halfway around the world. We might complain more about the poor quality of the picture on the plasma TV we just bought (for an exorbitant amount of money) than the fact that the images on the TV are depicting starvation and worldwide hunger. I'm not saying we shouldn't reap the benefits of our hard work, but we should keep things in true perspective and make some attempt to remember our personal responsibility in changing the conditions in the world. One person, standing alone, does not make a great impact on world situations, but many individuals with a joined purpose can make a difference.

Soul play:

+ Pick a topic—religion, politics, relationships ... anything you want. What are your current beliefs about this subject? Who influenced your beliefs?

+ Open yourself to the possibility that there is more to learn. Open your mind to the idea that another view might be more loving, peaceful, and forgiving. If you find you are resisting opening your mind, try to evaluate what is preventing you. How valid are your reasons? Are they based on fear or love?

+ Be courageous! Take another viewpoint and imagine for a moment that it is true. How does this perspective or view feel? Read your compass ... peace, love, and forgiveness. Does the new concept point in this direction?

+ How would accepting this new belief influence your life or the life of others? Would others be upset with you if you choose to believe something new? Does this prevent you from accepting it? Should it?

+ Once you have explored a new concept, you can choose to accept it for your own or release it, with thanks for the opportunity to have explored. If others have helped in teaching you about unfamiliar concepts, remember to thank them for their time, but do not allow them to "guilt" you or pressure you into continued pursuance of a subject you are not ready to accept.

Patience

Patience is the ability to keep an eternal perspective through the refinement of expectations. While expectancy can be a wonderful way toward the results we desire, there is the need for patience while awaiting the outcome.

There is also the need to understand that the outcome we expect may not be in accordance with what we or another was meant to experience in this life. We must let go of attachment to the outcomes and trust that all things will occur in their own time.

Enjoy the process! Life's twists and turns, which we may perceive as veering us off track, are the very paths we were meant to take. These "unplanned" and oft-times annoying deviations from the expected are those that teach us a great deal.

As in the knitting of a blanket, or the writing of a book—why should we become frustrated because we must move the needle or write a word? Every action we take brings us closer to our true path. Relax into the process and trust in the outcomes. If your blanket ends up becoming a scarf or your book turns out to be a poem—it doesn't mean that you failed. It means you were meant to knit the scarf or write the poem.

Our expectations are the challenge, and this is where our focus may need to change to come into patience, especially concerning others. Who are we to determine the path or progression of others? Who is to say what mission they have come to complete? Perhaps one of their life purposes was to teach us patience and unconditional love. We are all doing the best we can given our circumstances, conditioning, and individual perspectives.

Remember—when we lose patience with another, we are usually seeing a shortcoming we recognize in ourselves. We must focus on our own path and be gentle with ourselves and others.

On a personal note:

As a mother, I have had ample opportunity to practice the concept of patience! As every parent knows, we have expectations about how our children should dress, how neat their room should be, what courses they should take in school, what they should be when they grow up, what the person they marry should be like ... the list is endless.

As a wife, I have also had expectations. Sundays should not revolve around football (nor should any other day of the week!); Saturdays are for fixing things around the house; emptying the garbage and changing the oil are "men's" jobs; my husband shouldn't smoke cigars or be happier to see the dogs than anyone else ... this list is endless too.

Just look at all the opportunities we have to practice patience! The more specific our expectations are, the more impatient we become. I have discovered that when I let go of the nitpicky expectations and focus less on the outcomes and more on the process of parenting and being a loving partner, I can experience more patience when expectations fall short.

My husband and my children are each individual, unique beings with their own agendas and their own expectations. I cannot change the fabric of who they are ... I can only adjust my response to them. By not "sweating the small stuff," I have been able to maintain relationships and actually have my children talk to me about important issues.

When my children have been at their crankiest (and trust me, it doesn't end when they turn eighteen!), if I remained focused on patience and avoided losing my temper, I could usually root out the cause of the real problem behind the behavior. This has been a vital factor behind keeping the lines of communication open.

So often our plans don't seem to work out as we expected, and we discover later that if this had not been the case, we would have missed out on something great. When I graduated from nursing school, all I wanted was to work in a hospital and learn every advanced skill possible. At the time, there was a rare nursing glut, with too many graduate nurses looking for work, and the hospitals were taking only experienced nurses.

I remember sobbing ... feeling so disappointed that I "had to" accept a job in a nursing home. As it turns out, my path was meant to take me down this road. As a director of nursing, I have so many opportunities to be creative and make a real difference in the lives of those we care for. I have discovered a true affinity for the elderly, with a respect for the lives they have led. I have great compassion for those who feel sadness over all they have lost. Had anyone told me that this would be the case when I lost out on the hospital position, I would have denied that this would have been my path. But my soul knew better when it planned my path!

Now I try more to go with the flow and be more open about where my journey is leading me. I trust that the outcome will be for my ultimate good and for the good of others, as long as I practice patience and try to see where I'm being guided toward.

Soul play:

+ Think of someone with whom you lose patience.
+ Think of a circumstance that disappoints or frustrates you.
+ Determine what your expectations are regarding this circumstance or person.
+ How can keeping an eternal perspective, letting go of outcomes, respecting and trusting in the process, and keeping an open heart help you to refine your expectations so that you might come into patience?
+ How does this change in perspective effect how you feel about the other, yourself, or the circumstance?
+ Write down your discoveries in your Soul Play journal.

Peace

Peace is a state of loving acceptance of the world and oneself, including imperfection. It is accepting and embracing the differences between each of us as unique expressions of individual beliefs. It is the acknowledging of the divine within others and within ourselves, regardless of differences.

Worldly peace cannot exist without the inner peace of individuals, nor can it exist without equal concern for inner peace of others. The ability to obtain and retain inner peace can be complicated. Physical and emotional barriers can be present, and we need each other to help break the barriers down.

When we encounter individuals who cannot accept imperfections or differences with love—those who lack inner peace—they are easy to recognize. They are the ones who speak in anger, hate others, kill or physically inflict harm, manipulate, steal or covet, enjoy contention and discord, belittle others, and so on. These individuals need assistance with healing to gain inner peace. While we may at first want to respond with "righteous" anger, this is not the path to inner or world peace. Anger is a response that further alienates us from this objective.

There are many who walk the earth lacking inner peace. There are many people who are in need of emotional or mental healing but are under-recognized, under-diagnosed, and underemphasized. Consider the most destructive humans ever to have walked the Earth. What if their pain, hurt, or mental illness were recognized, diagnosed, and treated at their onset? Would so many have suffered as a result of their life?

The emotional and mental healing of mankind must be prioritized and sought by the multitude for there to be worldwide peace. The study of the human brain has taken a backseat to interplanetary travel and the quest for new and improved weapons of mass destruction. Why do people place more importance on that which is outside of themselves than on that which lies within? For world peace, this focus needs to change. Without the knowledge to heal mental illness and emotional pain, much of the violence and discord in the world will continue.

On a personal note:

We cannot watch the news without seeing acts of hatred and violence. We cannot open a history book without reading about the same experiences. When my first child was born, I was sitting on the couch with her head nestled in the crook of my elbow while she happily displayed her new talent of holding her own bottle. The mindless game show I'd been watching ended, and as channel changers were not as widespread as today, I was stuck for a while with whatever came on next.

A news story was beginning and warned that the contents were disturbing and discretion was advised. Mildly alarmed but unwilling to disturb my daughter, I watched the story unfold about the leader of a country who was in the process of committing genocide upon his own people with mustard gas. If the words of the report were not horrific enough, they ran a videotape of the streets of a town. I could not believe my eyes … mothers were lying on the ground with babies in their arms, still and lifeless, eyes open in terror.

The person operating the camera lingered on one baby, and his blanket had been thrown open when he and his mother had fallen to the ground and died. Through eyes streaming with tears I noticed his little legs … I was struck by the familiarity of the fat rolls on his thighs below his cloth diaper. He was about the same age as my daughter, and as I realized this, I looked down at her on my lap. My tears had landed and gathered in similar little rolls on her thighs, and she had stopped drinking her bottle to look at me. Had circumstances been different, that could be my baby lying dead in the street. Had I been born in that country, I could be the one running away in terror from those who were trying to kill us.

I gathered my daughter up and held her so tightly, thankful for our security, and grieving for the mothers and children, grandparents, and fathers who had died in that town. I struggled to make sense of who could inflict such a thing on another human being. The more I tried, the less sense it made. No well-adjusted, mentally healthy human being could do that to another. The answer was simple, and yet as complicated as the human brain. Those who do such things are not healthy. They are ill, and as a result, the symptom is destruction. The disheartening part was the realization that not enough research was being done to heal these people, and the madness would continue. This remains true today. When will we learn?

As I sat on my couch that day crying, with my baby in my arms, I hated the people who murdered the families in that town. I hated them so much I couldn't speak past the lump in my throat. I wanted them killed in the same way they murdered the innocent. More ... I wanted them to suffer first! But when I considered the nature of mental and emotional illness, and viewed those who committed such acts from this perspective, I could at least understand what causes such things to happen. I still wanted them to suffer, don't get me wrong! But I wanted the suffering to be a deep, searing regret for their own actions. I wanted them to understand and feel a healing pain for the hurt they had inflicted. And this could only come if there was a way to heal them.

Soul play:

+ Consider someone in history notorious for the harm he or she caused other human beings. Research that person's life and look for causes of emotional imbalance. When did he or she first demonstrate destructive behavior? How did this person choose to express the symptoms of his or her illness? Who was it directed at and why?

+ Imagine that through science, research, and/or love, society had been able to heal this individual and assist him or her gain inner peace. Imagine the way history would have played out differently ... imagine the course lives would have taken had they been free of the harm this individual caused. What outcomes would have been different? These can be far reaching—remember the ripple effect of actions.

+ Choose a group of people to do this exercise with. Each selects a different person in history. Meet together to discuss how history would have changed and how the present might have been effected.

+ Is there someone of your own acquaintance who might be healed with love or professional help? What can you, personally, do to facilitate this?

+ Write to your congressman to encourage support of research programs into the study of the human brain and mental illness. Encourage others to do so as well.

Playfulness

————————— 🌳 —————————

Playfulness is our spirit's way of loosening our hearts and minds to open up our creative circuits so new ideas can flow. When we open to a playfulness of spirit, we come to an understanding that all of life is play. By doing so, we can choose to lighten up the mundane and difficult.

When we match play with our passions, life becomes a joyous expression. Some of us don't explore play as a means of self-expression and have been programmed to believe that playfulness is "devil's work" or unproductive at best. Playfulness is not unproductive at all! In fact, the opposite is true. When we play and enjoy downtime, it allows our intellect to breathe, rest, and rejuvenate. Neglecting our need to play can result in drying up our creative energy. The mind is like a muscle that fatigues with overexertion. When it is allowed to recover its energy, it will be able to master a heavier load.

We must, however, maintain a balance. Too much time spent in leisure activity can, paradoxically, stunt our creative edge. Excessive play can become compulsive and avoidance-based, and lower our motivation. With respect to balance, extremes should be avoided.

In addition to respecting our own need for play, we must respect and encourage others as well. While some of us may benefit from another's tireless work, we need to understand that we would all benefit far more from a little playtime. By encouraging ourselves—and each other—to release and spend time at play, we become more productive, healthier, and happier human beings.

On a personal note:

You are talking to the queen of play! If there is anything I know how to do, it's find a multitude of ways to distract myself! Unfortunately, I have a tendency to take a good thing to extremes. When I find something I enjoy, I do it … eat it … drink it … play it … to the point that it starts to nauseate me. This is what I meant about avoiding excess. Too much of a good thing isn't necessarily good!

I am compulsive by nature, even in my work. There are times when I have been so involved in my work that I run out of creative or productive juice. That is when play has become an important rejuvenating element, instead of an avoidance tool. It is healthy to have a balance of work and play. I find that if I have music playing in the background while I am working, I enjoy the process more ... and this combination of work and play improves my productivity.

I would love for my husband to spend his days off working around the house fixing or building things. Some men and women actually consider this playtime for them! Unfortunately, I have not been so blessed: Michael's passion is the drums. From the time he was little, Michael was a frustrated drummer—tapping on anything he could get his hands on—counters, dashboards, his belly/chest/legs—and mourned the drummer he might have been. When he was little, his mom gave him a single drum at Christmas. The noise was so obnoxious that his parents banished him to the porch (in the bitter cold, to hear Michael's version!). For some reason ... I can't fathom why ... his solitary drum disappeared by New Year's! A part of him never got over it.

Although Michael and I hadn't exchanged presents since the kids were babies, I remember a special Christmas when we made an exception. I'd saved secretly for months and had Michael's brother, John, go with me to a music store to pick out a professional set of drums and cymbals. John set them up in the basement of my mom's house, and we put a big red bow on them, keeping them secret until Christmas morning. I fooled him by wrapping various sized boxes and putting them under the tree. In each box was an index card with a letter written on it. The first box revealed a D, the second an R, and so forth. He was completely perplexed, wondering what the heck I was doing. When he got to U, I could see it on his face ... the dawning of realization. He looked up, bug-eyed, and with his mouth dropped open, he whispered, *"No way!"* Then he tore into the next box, M, and the next, S ... and he looked at me with disbelief. I took his hand and led him downstairs, and he was just screaming with excitement. The kids were jumping up and down, and he was reverently touching the cymbals (apparently his brother was right when he said Michael would flip for Zildian cymbals).

Michael proceeded to play quite a bit with his drums (much to my dismay and chagrin), and at first I despaired that any work would be accomplished at home. But eventually, he found a balance … with a little limit setting … and became even more productive as a result. That man can accomplish any task as quick as a wink when he sees a carrot (or a beer) at the end of the stick!

Soul play:

+ Become aware of when you are in need of a little bit of downtime. Usually, your body knows before your mind … your neck muscles will begin to ache, your legs feel cramped and in need of stretching, and a mild headache may be present.

+ Play music while you are working … any kind that uplifts your spirit.

+ Stop working and give yourself permission to take a break to do something enjoyable. The more physical, the better!

+ If you see someone you work with getting cranky, encourage him or her to take a "play break." Watch productivity improve as a result.

+ Explore fun things to do or try. See how many fun things you can think of to fit into fifteen-minute blocks of time.

+ Reminisce about when you were a child. What things did you like to play? Hide and seek? Try to find an adult equivalent … like paintball! Did you collect Barbie dolls? Try Simms games on the computer. Use your imagination!

Power

Personal power is a driving force fueled by passion. It is the vehicle through which we accomplish our goals. This power is available through tapping into our Source. There is energy waiting to assist us to manifest what we desire. This power is infinite and available to all who seek to use it for the betterment of self and others.

Tapping into this power requires that we ask for it. We must let the Source know of our intentions and request divine assistance to provide universally directed energy. Power is God's will in action. When we align our will toward the good of all, we easily tap into this power because we are part of it.

Power over others is having the ability to influence them or to provide consequences to their actions. When we are in a position where we are responsible for determining justice in a situation, we would do well to remember that we should be deeply humbled by such a trust and ask for gifts of wisdom and compassion.

We may seek first to understand the mind and heart of those who may have caused offense. We may send them love and forgiveness, but this does not mean to shield them from the consequences of their actions. The natural law of cause and effect applies in all things. To protect others from this law is to deny them the growth they might require from the experience.

When power exists to influence others with words and actions, it is a sacred trust to be taken seriously. When used for the good of all, such power can be an awesome force. This is especially true when those we are teaching are shown the path toward their own power.

Power over others is a great responsibility, and we must exercise caution not to use it to manipulate or prevent another from exercising his or her own free will. The greatest power is one that respects choice and allows the natural law of cause and effect to prevail.

On a personal note:

I find that when I become consciously aware of the individual moments of my life, I have my finger on the pulse of my own personal power. It is when I notice the seemingly insignificant events or conversations of my day that I discover my ability to direct these events ... or at least control my responses to them.

It is not unusual for a day to go by where we are thrown from one set of circumstances into another, and we wonder what on Earth happened to the list of things we wanted to accomplish! We start to lament that we are tossed by fate into being a puppet to everyone else's priorities. A great phrase I heard once was, "Procrastination on your part does not equal an emergency on my part." We have to guard ourselves against rescuing other people from their own consequences and make our decisions based on our own agenda.

Often, however, as we are thrown into the ebb and flow of our days ... if we take a moment to become consciously aware and choose to guide the current, we can influence the direction of the course of events toward our overall goals. If we become too caught up in the energy and goals of others, rather than stay focused on our own vision, we may feel helpless and frustrated. With conscious awareness of our own choices, we are never helpless.

When others direct negative energy toward us, whether they are yelling or saying things to upset or demean us, it is empowering to remember that we have the ability to refuse to accept that negativity. We have the choice to become aware of our innate power to direct our own response! Rather than become upset and caught up in the negativity, we can notice how silly the others look with their faces pinched up. We can state firmly and without agitation that we are leaving the room until the other people calm down. We can decide that no matter how hard they try to blame us for their own upset, we refuse to accept the blame.

Our own vision of ourselves can have great power, so we must be aware of our own "self talk." Some of us don't need someone else directing negative energy toward us or blaming us when we are doing it to ourselves! Perhaps it's our own inner voice that we have to firmly direct to shut up! We can be our own harshest critic. This is the most dangerous kind of criticism, because we are often not even aware of the messages we are sending ourselves. When we send uplifting visions and thoughts to ourselves, our power is being utilized to create the person and circumstances we want. It all starts with awareness.

Soul play:

+ Consider those you have authoritative power over. In the past, how have you handled misconduct or breaking of rules? Were there natural consequences to breaking these rules (the kind the universe provides), or were they decided by you?
+ Examine your rules: Do they make sense? Are they for the good of all? Are there exceptions to the rule? What are they? Do those expected to live by these rules understand them?
+ Examine your consequences: What are they? Do they fit a natural cause and effect pattern? In other words, does the punishment fit the crime? Are there degrees of consequences? Do those who follow the rules understand the consequences for breaking the rules? Do they agree that the consequences are fair?
+ If you are in a position to influence others (and every parent is!), do you use this power wisely? Is your ultimate intent to maintain your own influence or to assist others to find their own inner wisdom and power?
+ Notice today the messages you send yourself. Catch your own self talk and observe whether you are sending empowering and positive visions to yourself or not. Redirect the type of messages into positive ones, and observe the response within yourself and those around you.
+ Become aware of the messages of others. If they are directing negativity toward you or blaming you, remember that you have the ultimate choice to block their energy and focus your mind on positive and uplifting thoughts.

Purification

———— ✣ ————

Purification is the process of cleansing. It is the emptying of the old to allow space for the new. Purification is necessary periodically and is a continuous process of clearing the way for renewal. The three main areas of focus are the triad of mind, body, and spirit.

When purifying the mind, we may use the cleansing properties of meditation. Meditation empties the mind of thoughts and allows us to free ourselves of our ego. There are many ways to prepare to meditate, and there are those of us who are intimidated that perhaps we may not do it "correctly." Concerning ourselves with technique will only serve to cause anxiety. Meditation is simple. It requires only that we relax the body and focus on being the observer of our thoughts as they come and go, without judgment, and lengthen awareness on the space between the thoughts. The more we practice meditation, the longer we can tune into the fluid-like quality of the space between our thoughts where all possibilities exist.

To purify the body, we may use the cleansing properties of water. Water is one of our body's main components, required for all bodily functions. It is a vital cleansing agent. As our body ages, our thirst drive diminishes, but our body's need for water does not. To cleanse the body of toxins, we must flush it with this life-giving substance. For three days, eat complex carbohydrates as close to their natural form as possible, and only when the body is truly hungry. Drink only water during these three days … at least two liters a day. Gently stretch your muscles each morning and evening, beginning with your core muscles … the largest ones close to your trunk. Move outward to include every muscle … finally to focus on your fingers, toes, and facial areas. Feel the body release negative energy and toxins while you stretch. Do not stretch to the point of pain as this is not beneficial to the body.

To purify the spirit, we may seek to experience our connection with our Source. In doing so, we must believe that we are worthy and capable of this connection. We can acknowledge that we are imperfect beings seeking connection with perfection. Self examination is helpful in preparing, but self-forgiveness is crucial in purification. Often we are harder on ourselves for our mistakes than we are on others. We must be gentle with ourselves and forgive our own imperfections as we seek to make wiser choices. We need to allow ourselves to feel worthy to connect in spirit with the Source.

Self-forgiveness propels us toward our Source, and the intention of connection draws our Source toward us. Allowing ourselves to open closes the gap, even though this gap is only a paradigm in our own minds. In truth, we are never separated from our Source. We must open our hearts to change this paradigm and acknowledge this spiritual connection. We may feel this connection as an absolute feeling of peace and calm … or with joy filling us to the point that tears fill our eyes and tingling warmth permeates our body. There is no right or wrong way to feel this connection.

On a personal note:

I am in perpetual need of purification! A lot like my house can become a mess with clothes and dishes and dust built up, my mind, body, and soul become littered with negative energy. Every once in a while … less often than I should … I detoxify. I will take the time in the morning to meditate and exercise, releasing tension and racing thoughts. I take the time to just "be" within myself. My body and mind feel as if a weight has been lifted.

Just as we end up with a cluttered house if we don't keep it up on a continual basis, when we are not vigilant with purifying our lives, the negative energy builds up, resulting in anxiety and discontent. Most of us wait until we feel the symptoms of anxiety before we begin the purification process. Pain is a potent motivator. But we don't have to wait to be in pain (physical, emotional, or spiritual) to purify. If we choose, we can opt for a maintenance plan of action instead.

If my feet ever start to swell, I know I'm retaining water. Ironically, water is the key to getting rid of the excess water in my body. I know that if I drink a lot of water, my body will detect that there is an abundance and release what it's holding. We have an ancient defense mechanism built into our systems that conserves what the body feels it may not get enough of. If the body detects an abundant inflow of water, it doesn't have a need to hold onto it. I still have to figure out how to convince my body not to hold onto fat! It doesn't seem to work in that department ... the more fat I feed myself, the more my body just holds onto it!

Self-forgiveness is a wonderful purification process. When we do not feel good about ourselves, our self-talk is negative, and it works like battery acid on the spirit. We need to cut ourselves a break, admit we made a mistake, and let it go. This is very important to do before seek communion with our Source.

Soul play:

+ Set aside a time and place each day to meditate. Choose a place and time where you are least likely to be disturbed.
+ Do not worry about whether or not you are meditating "correctly." Just enjoy the quietness of body and mind and allow yourself to become the observer of your own thoughts ... your own breathing ... and the space between each.
+ Devote several days to cleanse your system with water. Drink ten to twelve eight-ounce glasses. When you are hungry, eat foods as close to their natural form as possible. Avoid processed sugars and caffeine. You may have some withdrawal symptoms, such as cravings, headaches, or diarrhea. This is evidence that the toxins are being cleansed ... so don't get discouraged. By day four or five, you will feel the benefits of the purification. The water intake helps minimize the withdrawal symptoms. (If you have a medical condition such as diabetes or kidney disease, check with your physician before making any dietary changes.)
+ Decide to connect your spirit with the Source. Spend some time examining those things that cause you to feel unworthy of such a connection. Be gentle and forgiving with yourself. Acknowledge your imperfections, and know that God loves you unconditionally. Remember that you are divine offspring of the Source, and you are not seeking to connect with an entity outside of yourself. The connection comes from within. Feel gratitude for this remembrance and reconnection.

Purpose

Purpose is the aim of fulfilling our life's mission. It is meeting the course we have set for ourselves and following the flow of our soul's intent.

Before we began this earthly adventure, we decided what we wanted to accomplish. For some of us, there was one purpose—for others, there were several. Those who return to spirit early in life are highly advanced souls who came briefly for the purpose of teaching valuable lessons and assisting others to find and follow their missions.

There are many who worry about somehow not finding their life's mission. This is a needless concern. The purpose of our lives will find us when we are ready. All we need to do is open our eyes while we experience our lives. Often we will feel a desire to follow a particular career, but this is not necessarily the case. Our mission may have little to do with our careers ... we can be fulfilling our mission by simply being a good listener, by being born with a handicap, by overcoming addiction, by learning self-respect, and so on.

The best way to determine whether we are being led to fulfill a particular purpose is by the recognition of a nagging sense that there is something we are supposed to be doing. Or we may have an empty feeling and need to fill it. This is called sacred discontent. When we are meant to pursue a path and have yet to acknowledge and do so, we become filled with restlessness and dissatisfaction. This is necessary in order for us to recognize that there is something we need to open our eyes to. It means the time is rife to pursue a path.

The compass we must carry on this journey is joy and peace. By focusing on what brings us joy, we come into alignment with our purpose. Being true to our path may, at times, risk placing our own needs above those of another. This must be done gently and with much kindness and love, but it must be done. What purpose does it truly serve self or others to avoid confronting the very issues that prevent our joy from unfolding?

On a personal note:

When I realized that we each have come to this earth with different purposes, it helped me see people in a new light. The very idea that we chose the circumstances of our lives before we were born was one of those mind-stretching ideas for me. This knowledge has given me a greater appreciation for every person's journey in life. My soul knew which life experiences and relationships would best provide growth opportunities and karmic settlements necessary for its progression. Our souls are eternal. We originated as part of the Source. We separated from Its perfection in order to be able to fully understand and appreciate what it meant to be a part of such paradise. We wanted to be able to become like the Source from which we originated—able to create our own joy and light. How can light shine without darkness? The contrast—the separation from our Light Source—was necessary so that we could learn to shine.

I took my children with me to volunteer to be a "friend for a day" at a fair at the community college, held in honor of mentally challenged children. We were each assigned one of these special children to take to the various booths to have faces painted, balloons tied to wrists, win prizes at games, and dance at the bandstand with them. With my newfound knowledge that these children and adolescents had chosen the handicap they were born with, I realized what a true honor we were given to be in the presence of such selfless, advanced souls.

We don't all have such magnified purposes here, but this doesn't make our journey less noble. I know that my purpose includes teaching and writing. I have felt a pull toward nursing as well. To follow my promptings toward my mission here, I have had to sacrifice a number of things, such as time, energy, money, and attention ... which might have otherwise gone to my family. They were, thankfully, understanding of my need to follow my path. Had they not been willing to sacrifice, it would have made it difficult to pursue my goals. But I would have had to continue despite their objections, because I know that these things were needed to bring me joy and a sense of purpose in my life.

This sense of purpose, and fulfilling a mission, has also helped me see my problems in a new light. I no longer ask, "Why me?" when something "bad" happens ... at least not in the same way. I would ask the question with self pity in a rhetorical sort of way before. Now I ask to discover the possible reasons I brought the circumstance into my life. I also look to determine, "Why me, now, at this time? What am I meant to learn from this? Where is this leading me? Who is it leading me toward and what role will they play in my life?"

Soul play:

+ Are you experiencing sacred discontent? Attempt to define this feeling by writing how it feels. Identify when you feel it most often. What events are happening, or people are present, when you feel this way? Place yourself in those moments in your mind's eye. What is missing? What do you yearn for? What would bring you joy?
+ Would others be affected by your pursuit of a path that would fulfill your need for peace and joy? How can you gently prepare them for the changes that may affect them?
+ How can your respect for nurturing your own needs teach them to respect themselves and prompt them toward their own paths?
+ Are you guilty of preventing someone else from following his or her path? How can assisting this person with his or her mission help fulfill your own?
+ Don't become frustrated by the feeling that something is missing from your life. Pray and focus on bringing your purpose toward you, and open your eyes for coincidences that will lead you toward living your life "on purpose."

Release

Release is letting go of the need to control people or situations and accepting that the course of events will unfold in their own way and time. It is ceasing to require power over outcomes.

There are times we feel that life is such a struggle and no one seems to want to cooperate with our view of how life should be. We may find the behaviors of another frustrating because they don't comply with our view of the correct order of things. From our ego-based perspective, all of these conditions need to be made right because we perceive them as wrong.

When we set aside the ego, we come to the understanding that the universe revolves around all of us, not just ourselves. We may perceive of the "correct thing" differently than someone else does. It is unlikely that creating a struggle with another will result in a change of his or her viewpoint. When we release the struggle and the need to be right, we open lines of respect and communication in order to come to an understanding of the other's viewpoint (even if we don't agree with it).

Releasing certain negative emotions lightens our spirit. Holding on to anger, bitterness, hatred, the need for revenge, and so on, creates a heaviness of heart and a block of the flow of positive energies. We must be willing to accept that these emotions serve us no useful purpose—regardless of why we hold them or how justified we feel to do so. We can release these feelings with love and forgiveness. In fact, there is no other way to truly release them. Without love and forgiveness, we are simply storing the acidic feelings away for later, and they will fester in our soul.

When we send out an intention or a prayer, we must release our attachment to the outcome. If a seed is planted, it will grow when and in whatever manner the universe chooses. Releasing the need to control the process creates a much happier outlook on life and allows inner peace to flourish.

On a personal note:

My husband, Michael, and I have had our share of ups and downs ... most of which are centered around his need to always be "right" in any situation. In art class in high school, my son created a pottery mug and inscribed "I'm right, you're wrong—end of discussion" as a gift for his father.

Before I learned to release my need to "make him see the light" and sway him to my way of thinking, my efforts to do so resulted in endless arguments and hard feelings. The harder I tried to convince him of my viewpoint, the firmer he would dig in his heels on the issue. The more I tried to convince him he was wrong, the more he felt the need to prove himself right. In fact, if I began to prove one of my points correct, he would get all the more agitated and determined to justify himself. People, in general, do not want to be proven wrong or incorrect in their thinking. It becomes a matter of pride.

I have discovered the serenity of the philosophy "to each his own." I have released the struggle of trying to prove anyone wrong. I can, instead, comment that I understand their viewpoint ... even if I disagree. I have learned the art of agreeing to disagree on certain issues. This release has gone a long way in making our home more peaceful!

Releasing a prayer into the universe, especially in stressful situations, can bring such welcome relief! If we become like nagging children, begging over and over for the same thing, it sends out a clear message of distrust that our request will be answered to our satisfaction. Prayers are like seeds, and the answers may take time to cultivate. The flower it produces may not always resemble the one we expected, but it is always the one we were meant to grow.

I was driving home from work one bitterly cold evening when a white blur in the middle of the highway caught my eye. I realized it was a kitten, sitting on the road's divider line, with cars zooming on either side of it. I pulled over, got out of my car, and proceeding to stop traffic dead on Route 9 while I rescued it. As I picked the kitten up, I could feel him shaking from cold and fright. His nose was bleeding slightly, which I knew could indicate a brain injury. Someone realized my plight and assisted me to get help to take him to the animal hospital where they gave him steroids to decrease potential swelling in the brain. He had a broken hip and was apparently blind either from a birth defect or from the impact of the car. The doctor said there was nothing else to do.

So I took my little bundle home and spent the rest of the evening picking off fleas, washing off blood, and praying. After about two hours of praying, I began to feel redundant, like I was whining! Although I wanted him to be okay, I had to release the outcome to what was meant to be. I accepted that even if the poor thing died, I had done my best. As providence would have it, he gradually began to eat and then to walk. I taught him to use the litter box, and worried if he'd find it again, because he was still blind. I knew we were blessed when he began to growl as the dogs came into the room and he seemed to follow them with his eyes. His sight fully returned, but he was very unhappy to see those dogs! I was heartbroken to let him go, but for his sake I gave him to a friend. He is now the king of their house, and is fat, happy, and healthy!

Soul play:

+ Identify a situation in which you have been struggling for control. Has your need to be right or in control alienated another or made you anxious?
+ Identify a person with whom you have argued. Have you been trying to control his or her behaviors or prove the person wrong? Release the need to be right. Release your judgment of right versus wrong. Observe how your change in behavior produces new responses in yourself and the other involved.
+ Choose an experience that resulted in angry and bitter feelings. On the left side of a piece of paper, write down the name of the person and any key words to describe the negative feelings eating at you. Draw an arrow toward the right side of the paper and write the words "forgiveness, peace, and love." Take a flame and burn the paper, symbolically releasing the negative emotions. Imagine them dissipating as the smoke rises. Envision them rising to be healed by the universe. Allow yourself to feel the peace this release brings. Symbolism is a powerful tool into our subconscious and is useful in releasing. (Just be safe—use caution and a non-flammable container ... and avoid windy days if you are practicing this exercise outside!)
+ Say a prayer and specifically state your request . Then do not ask again!

Responsibility

Responsibility is the ability to respond to the events in our lives and world with integrity. It is the acceptance, as well, that we are in control of our responses.

Personal responsibility involves not blaming others for the conditions in our lives. Not our parents, spouses, children, or anyone besides ourselves are to blame for our problems with addiction, depression, anger, poverty, or other afflictions. When we blame another, we render ourselves powerless. Why do we do this? Because it is easier to believe someone else is in control. It gives us an excuse not to act and risk failure. For if another is responsible to begin with, how can we hope to change on our own? Powerlessness becomes an excuse to not act with integrity.

Blaming circumstances for our responses to them is another way of rendering ourselves powerless. When we choose the idea that we are not in control of our actions, we avoid taking responsibility for them. We are free to respond with anger or the need for revenge or a myriad of other negative emotions and convince ourselves that we are justified. After all, weren't we just reacting to the actions of the other? If we react without consciously choosing our response, we are relinquishing responsibility from acting with integrity. This leads to negative outcomes.

Worldly responsibility involves understanding that every individual can, in some small way, influence the world for its good. By being the example, perhaps others may follow. Something as simple as bending down to pick up litter on the ground sets the tone to invite others to do the same. Prayers for the well being of other countries are just as important as those for our own. Do not underestimate the power of prayer in influencing peace.

When we avoid taking responsibility for our lives, we are easily influenced by others and become caught up in a cycle of helplessness. When this occurs, we are allowing others to choose our paths. This leads to frustration and lack of peace. This is sacred unrest, because we must learn to direct our own lives. We can regain our power by accepting responsibility.

On a personal note:

It's so much easier to blame someone else. "I want to lose weight, but he keeps bringing chips into the house." "I'm yelling because I'm just reacting to what she did." "I'm so depressed ... he never pays attention to me." "Why should I pick up that gum wrapper? He just walked right by it!" "I hit my kids because that's the way my parents handled discipline problems." "I'm a psychological mess because my father never paid enough attention to me."

Anytime there is something we need to improve, if we haven't yet, we explain it by putting the word "because" after it and then name someone else as the reason why!

Why is it so hard to believe "the buck stops here"? Just because someone else did or did not do something does not give us the go ahead to blame them for our reactions. Yes, maybe this person did all the things you accuse him of, but you are the one who decides how you will react to it.

When the kids were transitioning into those lovely teenage years, and they decided that every word out of my mouth was an opportunity to begin an argument, I spent many a day aggravated and hoarse from yelling to be heard. I was reacting to their irritating need to contradict everything I said. Then one day, I just got it ... like a lightbulb going off in my head! I didn't have to react to their comments with anger or defensiveness! I could choose to remain centered and calm in the face of idiotic comments, even when they were said to elicit a rise out of me! When I realized this, the cycle of negative interaction stopped dead in its tracks. There was no one to argue with. The funny thing was that when I ceased trying so hard to be heard, I was able to listen a little more. This makes for much more productive relationships.

The "chips" scenario is mine. My husband, Michael, nurtures his family with food. He loves nothing better than to bring home a bag of refreshments and watch the glow of appreciation from his family. He also doesn't like to have us suggest that he run back to the store, so he makes sure he brings a few goodies home. Well, 99.9 percent of the time we are all very happy with this arrangement. But when we decide that we are dieting and the chips come through the door, it is Michael's fault that our diets are out the window! Unreasonable? Yes! Do I do it? Yes! I'm learning that the buck stops at my lips if I want to diet. There will always be delicious-smelling bakeries to pass by … I can't blame the baker for baking!

Soul play:

+ What condition in your life are you blaming someone else for?
+ Identify the choices you have made (or have not made) that led you to this condition.
+ Identify how and when you gave up your power.
+ Make a decision to acknowledge that you are responsible for every condition in your life. Write down what you have done, or chosen not to do, to lead you to your current state of affairs.
+ How have your responses affected the people around you? How have they affected you? If your responses had been different, what might the outcomes have been?
+ How can accepting responsibility change your perspective and help you reclaim your power?

Simplicity

Simplicity is a state of being where you realize that all you are is all you need. It is the state of having released the many wants and "have tos" in one's life—to have more, be more, taste more, drink more, and so on. It is the joy in knowing that this moment is all there is and being content seeking the meaning within it.

Releasing attachment to the excesses in our lives leads to simplicity. This does not mean we need to give all of our possessions away or stop enjoying life! It means releasing the idea that somehow these things complete us or are part who we are. No one truly owns anything, in a spiritual sense. Place value on the things that can't be taken away—love, knowledge, creating meaningful experiences, and so on. Focusing on these will help us release attachments that distract us from what is important, and this will empower us.

Consider a straight path—we can see clearly from where we are standing to the place we want to be. We begin to walk the path and take notice of many unnecessary branches that we know lead to dead ends, but we think we are required to explore each of them. Soon we find so many dead end paths we lose sight of the one that leads us to our destination. Simplicity releases the need to explore the unnecessary and gives us clearer vision.

It is difficult to hear that which is meaningful when there is a lot of senseless chatter surrounding us. Removing clutter from our mind and taking a few minutes each day to empty our thoughts, to focus on nothing more than the breaths we take helps us find simplicity and clarity. Quiet meditation helps redirect our minds toward more meaningful channels.

On a personal note:

This is one of those concepts where I could benefit from listening to my own advice! I yearn for simplicity in my home, yet I'm a collector. My husband calls me the "yard sale queen," because I have to stop at every garage sale I see, *knowing* I'll find something great … really cheap. As a result, I have accumulated a lot of stuff. Stuff on shelves in the basement, stuff at the top of my closet, stuff cluttering my kitchen cabinets …

So, every year I have to weed through my stuff, put aside the "don't needs," and give them to charity. Even so, I find it difficult to part with my useless stuff. Why is this? There is always the nagging thought that "someday" I may need that extra bowl, or I'll have time to use those craft materials, or I'll actually use that foot massager … yes, *eeeww*, I actually bought a used foot massager no one in my house will use …

Why do I horde? Most likely it's because somewhere in my mind I suffer from a sense of lack. I live in a world of my own making that believes I need these things "just in case." They sit, in closets, unused for months or years, because I might have a need for them "someday." Then I complain that there isn't enough space in my closet for the stuff I use every day!

When I consider that I am all I really need, and that the universe is a giving and generous place, it is easier to let go of the unnecessary things. This includes thoughts. So often, I used to torture myself with thoughts of self-doubt, insecurity, and fear. These thoughts clutter the mind so much that there is not much room left for productive thoughts. Releasing these useless, negative thoughts simplifies the flow toward a more useful, positive mindset. I have learned that getting rid of the negative clutter has made me a much happier person … even if I am still learning not to buy old foot massagers!

Simplifying our schedules is another way toward a more peaceful existence. These days, we expect ourselves to be able to "do it all"—spend time with the family, be a loving partner, be successful at work, spend time with our extended families, spend time with friends, go to the gym (yeah, right!), go to church, volunteer for community projects—the list is endless.

We need to learn to say *no*! politely, but loudly and clearly. Set limits as to who or what is allowed to clutter your schedule. Leave yourself time for filling the cup of your soul first … all else is secondary! If watching the sunrise fills your cup, do it. If reading from an inspiring book fills your cup, do it. Do whatever makes you happy first, and then pencil in everything else, in order of its importance in adding to your happiness. Simplify!

Soul play:

+ What excesses do you have in your life?
+ What unnecessary dead-end paths have you chosen to experience?
+ What things or ideas are you attached to, and what belief do you hold that without them you are incomplete?
+ How can understanding that "you are already all you really need" assist you in releasing attachments to things outside yourself?
+ The next time your thoughts become confused or cause upset, take ten minutes to refocus by clearing your mind of thoughts and concentrate simply on the process of breathing in and out.
+ Ritualistically make a pile of "stuff" in your home that you haven't used in a year. Give it to the needy.
+ What negative or pessimistic thoughts clutter your mind? Get rid of them! Replace them with positives!
+ What does your daily and weekly schedule look like? Do you leave no time for things that bring you joy? Monitor your schedule, how you spend your time, for one week. What can you change or eliminate to simplify your schedule to open up time for the things that make you happy?

Spontaneity

Spontaneity is acting upon the impulse to set aside routine and do that which comes to mind naturally. It is the freedom to act in the moment.

There is always a time we feel a strong impulse to do something. We might get the urge to call someone we haven't spoken to in years, to hug someone and tell her she's loved, to take a drive to the beach, to fall backward onto a pile of leaves, to pick up a book, to walk a new path, and so on. We are being prompted toward something when we get these urges.

We must become aware when these impulses come and accept what we are being directed toward, even if their purpose is a moment's joy or a peaceful interlude. Often we get so caught up in the details of our lives that there is no time for spontaneity. We have the kids to drive, meetings to get to, bills to pay, houses to clean, lawns to mow, shopping to do … a never-ending list of tasks. We become so habitual in our routines that we lose touch with our spontaneous nature.

When we are inflexible with our routine, we miss out on opportunities to experience joy and revelation. It is not the things we do that we most regret at the end of our life. It is, rather, the missed opportunities to follow our heart's desire we mourn. We need to be willing to leave the dust on the furniture for a few more days and follow the impulse to feel the sand between our toes, or to spend the afternoon at the bookstore feeding our minds. The dust will wait. The lawn will wait. Life is calling!

Many of us are afraid that if we act spontaneously, we might appear irresponsible or silly. So what? Who cares if someone raises an eyebrow to our play? More often than not, others will wish they could join in! Our routines and expected behaviors rule our lives a great percentage of the time. We are allowed to enjoy spontaneity when we are so inclined. Then we can look back at our life when we are old and remember all the fun we had, all the people we met, all the things we learned, and the places we saw!

We will be able to say we spent our time doing things that provided joyful memories.

On a personal note:

We all would do well to release our self-consciousness, to "let go" once in a while, and stop worrying so much about appearances. I had an opportunity to do just that when my husband and I went on a little getaway to the Helmsley Park Lane Hotel in New York City. It was way out of our budget, and a total indulgence … to live as the wealthy do for a day.

Our room was on the forty-first floor and all of Central Park was laid out before us … ice skaters, Central Park Zoo, Belvedere Castle, Tavern on the Green, fields, paths, ballparks … and the homes of the rich and famous lined all sides of it! The architecture along the rooftops alone was inspiring. Below on the street were the horse-drawn hansom cabs lining the cobblestone curbs. Michael and I took a turn on them, and it was very cozy … clip-clopping along the path with a red velvet blanket over our legs.

We left the hotel to go to our Broadway show and the regal doorman formally opened the door and prepared to hail a taxi for us. There were two distinguished-looking gentlemen ahead of us waiting for one as well. All of a sudden, this rickshaw-like contraption pulls up (a little wagon seat, pulled by a bicycle) … and its very skinny driver proclaimed loudly, "Fastest way to Broadway! Hop in!" To which the two men in front of us looked the other way, and Michael chimed in, "You think those skinny little legs can haul the two of us?" Now, the two gentlemen slowly turned to look at us two fatsos and cracked a grin. Before I had time to punch Michael in the face, he was pulling me toward this wagon and pushing me into it. I was torn between laughter and yelling there was *no way* I was climbing in but found the two of us stepping up into the carriage while Michael called out, "I hope you don't charge by the pound!" The two gentlemen disintegrated into helpless laughter, and so did Michael and I, curious to see if this guy's skinny little legs could handle the task!

So off we went, and the little guy was true to his word. We were weaving in and out of traffic, cutting off the taxis (if you ever rode in a taxi in New York, you can imagine the danger being multiplied by a hundred!). I was trying to bury my head under Michael's shoulder to be as inconspicuous as possible, but our driver would have none of it as he hollered at every corner, "Fastest way to Broadway!" Going through nearly red lights … across three lanes of traffic … obeying no rules! Then the poor guy turned down a block and Michael and I looked at each other, our eyes growing wider, and we both said, "Oh no! Uphill!" What a sight we must have been, with my previously styled hair blown all over the place, the two of us crammed into this little carriage, being hauled up the hill by a panting little man on a bike!

The poor man was coughing by the time he got to the top, and Michael and I were laughing so hard we were crying. It was the fastest way to Broadway, as promised, and we gave him a *very* generous tip! I hadn't laughed that hard in a long time! And if I hadn't allowed myself to let go of pretenses and self-consciousness, I would have missed the experience.

Soul play:

+ What is your weekly routine? Do you clean and shop or mow the lawn on Saturdays? If you have the urge to take a walk through the park or on the beach—go! Don't force yourself to always stick to your routine. Open yourself to spontaneity.
+ Prioritize, for a change, the impulse to do the unusual. Break your routine.
+ Do not allow yourself, or anyone else, to make you feel guilty or silly to be spontaneous. Self-consciousness can ruin anyone's good time!
+ Become aware of when the urge to do something heartfelt and spontaneous hits. Try to determine why this urge came to mind. Is there possibly a deeper meaning to the urge? Perhaps your child really needed that spontaneous hug and words of love!

Strength

Strength is the power to endure, withstand, and overcome the trials and tests that present themselves in our lives. It is the ability to stay firmly rooted in the Source while the winds of change and storms of fear surround us.

Strength requires flexibility and, at times, bending our view of how life is "supposed" to play out. It is one of the qualities we have come to earth to learn. As in building a muscle, the development of strength requires opposition.

We must not look at the trials and obstacles of our lives as awful. This impedes our actions. We must stand back from our emotional responses long enough to observe them as the instructional tools they represent. From an objective standpoint, one that recognizes that in reality, the soul is always safe, we are better able to seek solutions from a rational perspective.

Make no mistake, there is no problem presented to us that does not hold, inherent within itself, a solution. We must diligently seek this solution for ourselves, as this process strengthens our spirit. If we are unable to find the solution, we should seek out others who are better equipped to do so. We can ask for assistance from our Source in this endeavor.

There is strength in unified purpose. The more a group consciousness focuses on the solution to a problem, the more rapidly the solution will present itself. Do not become caught up in ego, requiring that you be the only one to solve an issue. In building strength, the effort is what counts.

Strength requires fearlessness. We must not be afraid of outcomes. We must have faith in our ability to handle whatever will happen. We must also be willing to accept that a greater Will is at work in the universe and that the Source has all things in their proper order even if, from our limited perspective, we disagree with an outcome.

On a personal note:

It must be no coincidence that, as I sit to write this, providence would have it that my life is in the throws of the "winds of change and storms of fear." I have what the doctors mysteriously call a "mass" on my neck, which has begun to feel like a noose every time I move or swallow. I am scheduled this morning to go for a test that will help determine whether or not I have cancer, and I could not have chosen a better word than strength to inspire me. As always, I write about that which I need to learn!

I've been agonizing for the three weeks I have had to wait to take the test, imagining the worst, and probably talking myself into more symptoms. When I got an earache, the cancer had surely spread! The muscle twinge in my arm means it's all over my body! I even have my daughter convinced that I have to write her letters to open at important moments in her life, since I'll be dead. Does this sound like a woman of courage?

When I had written this essay on strength, I remember thinking, *This sounds great, but someone going through a life crisis might flip a middle finger at me!* After all, who was I to write about such things, when my life overall was relatively smooth sailing? Perhaps the experience I am going through, as frightening as it is, is the greater Will setting things into place in their proper order to inspire others. If nothing else, it's time to put my money where my mouth is and learn from my own words to find courage in handling the situation!

I do know, in my heart, that whatever the outcome today … I am held safe and secure in the arms of our Creator, and that my soul is always anchored. I also trust that whatever the long-term outcome of this process is meant to be, it has been designed for the benefit of my journey and for those who might be affected by it. I acknowledge that I was co-creator of the script of my life, and I will seek to be an expression of the courage I aspire to.

In the process of the struggles of life, I know that I become more of who I truly am. Like the butterfly in the cocoon, I am building strength in my wings that I might become what I am meant to be—an expression of the Source.

Soul play:

- When a trial or obstacle appears in your life (and it will!), recognize it as an opportunity to develop strength of spirit.
- Resist the temptation to be overcome or sidetracked by emotional response. Attempt to view the situation from an eternal mindset, and remind yourself that you are safe regardless of outcomes. This will help you release fear.
- Remind yourself that there is a solution to every problem inherent within itself.
- Ask the Source for assistance in resolving the problem. Examine the problem objectively from all sides and perspectives.
- Determine a solution and try it out. If this doesn't work, don't become discouraged … you have just ruled out one theory, so try another!
- If you have tried and cannot find the solution, you have not failed. You have learned what did not work. Seek out those who might help you. Teach them what you have tried which did not work, and use group discussions to seek solutions.
- Identify your sources of strength: family, friends, books, music, your community, church, support groups, prayer, etc. Don't be hesitant to accept help in your process … it does not mean you are weak.
- Write down your experience in your journal so that, when you encounter your next "bump" in the road of life, you can read about how you handled this one successfully.

Surrender

Surrender is the releasing of control over certain events in our lives, and acknowledging that the Source is in the driver's seat. When accomplished with trust, surrender is tremendously relieving.

Trust must be present when we release control to the Source. This trust requires that we release our interest in the outcome of a situation. There can be no surrender without this. Although we may feel otherwise when things "go wrong," this is not the case. Events are unfolding exactly as they should. Our soul knows the reason why certain events are occurring in our lives, even if we do not have access to this unlimited perspective here on earth. We may learn these reasons at some point in this lifespan, or we may need to wait until we are again in spirit for them to be revealed. Either way, we must trust that all things happen for a reason.

When we are in a situation where we have a strong attachment to an outcome, it can generate a great deal of anxiety. From this state of anxiousness, emotions such as fear, worry, anger, doubt, and so on, can become overwhelming and disabling. When we release (or surrender) the outcome, we are relieved of these negative emotions and are no longer paralyzed. In this sense, ironically, surrender is actually empowering!

On a personal note:

Surrender comes with difficulty to me. I like to feel as though I am control of every situation I face. I like to solve problems and wrap them up in neat little packages labeled "resolved." Unfortunately, unlike a lot of happy-ending-type books and movies, life is not always so conveniently predictable.

The more we have at stake in an outcome, the more difficult it is to "let go and let God." One of the things that matter to us the most is the health and wellbeing of our loved ones. When they suffer, we suffer. When we have no control over their suffering, we agonize. We beat against the door of fate until our hands bleed in our fight for control. Finally, we reach the point of exhaustion and begin to surrender. But it is the way we surrender that makes all the difference. It makes the difference in whether we experience our reality through depression or through hope.

When my son, Michael, was five years old, he had what I assumed to be an odd stomach virus. He vomited but never seemed to have the diarrhea that usually goes along with it. I was not in nursing school yet, and I had no clue what kind of problem this could indicate. Because he was not even able to hold down liquids, he was becoming dehydrated. I took him to the emergency room, but his pain and vomiting suddenly resolved, and we all thought everything was fine. The doctor warned me that since Michael had had surgery as a baby, scar tissue might have formed a "bow" around the bowel and could have obstructed it temporarily by tightening. He said to report any other symptoms immediately.

A week later, the same symptoms returned. This time, though, the pain was the most predominant issue, and we rushed him to the emergency room. I explained what the previous doctor had warned us of, and tests proved him right. Michael needed emergency surgery because his bowel was about to rupture, and this would cause peritonitis. I had only recently heard of peritonitis (a potentially deadly infection) when I'd been told that Heather O'Rourke, the beautiful little girl who had acted in the movie *Poltergeist*, had died from it.

While they were preparing for surgery, I had to rush home with my two other children and arrange for their care before speeding back to the hospital. I'll never forget that ride back to the hospital. My anxiety level was causing me to literally shake. I was praying the same thing over and over like a chant: "Please, God, let him be okay." I became almost disabled in my effort to drive. I was so afraid I was going to get to the hospital and be told, "I'm sorry, we lost him." I felt totally helpless. As I was stopped at a red light, strongly considering racing through it, I suddenly felt a palpable answer to my prayer. A voice in my mind said, "Everything is okay ... one way or another, everything is okay." I knew this didn't mean that Michael would live or die. It meant that regardless of the outcome, all things would be as they were meant to be, and his soul would always be okay. I heaved a huge sigh and could feel the tension drain from my body. I surrendered. I was then able to focus and function as I needed to.

As it turned out, it was not Michael's time to leave this Earth yet. But the outcome could have gone either way. I said the same prayer when my nephew suffered a brain aneurism. I wished for a miracle to save him. He was so young and had such a promising future ahead of him. Adam was the kind of guy who wasn't in a hurry to watch the football game after Thanksgiving dinner but would linger at the table and talk about a multitude of subjects and enjoy everyone's company. He was active and healthy and driven to improve the environment. How could such a vital person be fated to die so young? I don't know the answer to this question, because I don't have insight into what Adam's mission in this life was. One thing I do know is that it was his time to leave. If it wasn't, he would still be here. No amount of fighting against the course of events will change this fact. When we surrender, with trust, that everything will be okay in the end, it releases the anger and helplessness, even if it doesn't take away the pain.

Soul play:

+ When things are going wrong and you can feel your anxiety level building up to a crescendo, physically pause for a moment and take a deep breath. Give yourself permission to stop thinking momentarily about anything ... mentally say the command, "Stop!" Breathe deeply a few times during this mental pause while your body has a chance to stop producing fight-or-flight hormones.
+ Consider the outcome you are so anxious about. Acknowledge that there is a universal, spiritual plan we may not be aware of. Accept that this plan was created for the progression and mission of each soul involved in the circumstances. Accept that, in the end, everything turns out exactly as it was meant to.
+ Allow yourself to believe that, in the end, we will all be okay, from a spiritual perspective.
+ Take a deep, cleansing breath and surrender to this universal plan and trust in its ultimate wisdom.
+ Once this surrender occurs, you will feel more centered and able to think and direct your actions toward the outcome you desire.

Synthesis

Synthesis is the organized orchestration of the elements of creation. Sometimes these elements hit us like a baseball bat or a like a light bulb going off, but more often than not they are subtle.

We must recognize the parts of the whole and pull them together to manifest the creation. When an intention to manifest has been sent into the universe, many seemingly insignificant events will occur in our lives that will later prove key elements in our own creation. In order to bring these elements together, we must first become aware of their significance through consciously opening our eyes to events and people crossing our paths. We must determine how, or if at all, they fit into our intention.

Once there is recognition, we must decide how the element would best be utilized in the creation. For example, if your intention is to purchase a first home, when the name of an outstanding mortgage broker comes to you (and it will), you will need to decide how this information will be used. Will you "shelf" the name until you've straightened out your finances? Will you call just to ask questions, but not apply?

We need to understand that, in creating, the decision to act—to synthesize—is necessary. We must trust that if we have received a piece of the puzzle—such as the name of someone who might help us—we deny our own intention by inaction. We do well to remember there are no failures—there is only learning. The only thing we can equate to failure is deciding not to try at all … but even then, we are learning that inaction leads us nowhere.

To remove fear from the equation, we can ask ourselves, "What is the worst thing that could happen?" In the example of the purchase of a home, the worst-case scenario might be that the mortgage application is denied. This is not such an awful thing … our actions of the past may have led to this natural consequence. The key is not focusing energy on that and giving up—we must keep our thoughts focused on the intention, not on what may hold us back. We can ask the mortgage broker ways to repair our credit, and focus our attention on paying down high-interest debt. At least we learned how to move in the right direction, and this is empowering because it brings us one step closer to buying that house.

On a personal note:

When my husband and I were separating, the owners of the house I was renting became nervous about my ability to pay the rent and decided to sell the house. I had three children, each firmly established in school with their own friends. How could I pull them from the security of their friends when they were already dealing with the loss of their home and, in a sense, their father?

Yet every time I looked through the newspaper, I could not find a house in town to rent. I only had two months to find something, and I was beginning to lose hope. About this time, I was reading Wayne Dyer's book, *Manifest Your Destiny*, and thought, *Well, if ever there was a time I needed to manifest … this is it!* So I decided to give it a try, and asked, very specifically (because why bother at all if I couldn't ask for what I wanted) for a little blue house with a white porch in Spotswood, New Jersey. I dared the universe to come up with that one! And in two months!

I was open. Elements began coming together, and I jumped on them. My daughter's friend saw a clipping from a small local newspaper about a house for sale by owner. She had cut it out and given it to my daughter Jennifer. When Jenny brought the clipping to me, I said at first, "Jen, this person is selling their home, not renting it … how does this help me?" She questioned me about why I couldn't buy the house, but I did not believe it was possible. After all, hadn't my husband told me so enough times? Why bother trying?

So I decided I was going to try to talk the owners into renting with the option to buy, and I called for an appointment. As I pulled up in front of the house, I turned the ignition off and began laughing at the sight before me. Sitting right on the corner lot was a little blue house with a white porch … in Spotswood! Deciding this was a good omen, I knocked on the door. The owner was a warm, caring woman who also questioned why I couldn't purchase the house. She gave me the name of a wonderful mortgage broker and encouraged me to at least try. I was disappointed that I couldn't rent the house, but I called the broker that day. He held my hand through the whole application process, and guided me the entire way, understanding that I had never done this before. When I got the news that the mortgage was approved, my kids and I whooped and hollered with joy! All of the elements had synthesized together to make my house a reality!

Soul play:

+ Choose and send out an intention to manifest something in your life. Be as specific as you want.
+ Take a month to actively identify elements of creation sent into your life (even so-called bad events are keys).
+ Decide to act upon any leads you receive. This may include calling someone, writing someone, looking in the newspaper, making an appointment—whatever it is—do it! Action is the key!
+ Suspend doubt ... don't let your fear of failure or being wrong stop you from trying! Don't let negative people influence your decision to try!
+ Write events down in your journal ... seemingly unrelated events may take on a pattern or connection you might not otherwise have observed.

Tenderness

Tenderness is a state of being in which we have opened our protective shell and allowed gentle, vulnerable feelings to enter. As the earth softens and relaxes in the spring to allow rain to enter and nourish its seeds, so do we have the opportunity to release our hard crust. This openness allows for intimacy to bloom. It creates fertile ground for love to grow.

Without tenderness, there can be no true intimacy, for this requires sharing of feeling. Intimacy requires that we become vulnerable. Entering into this state can be fearful for some. They may have been hurt in the past or may have been conditioned to believe that softness is a sign of weakness. They may have decided that vulnerability is never an acceptable state.

Tenderness does leave us vulnerable and exposed—and it takes courage! However, even if another is unkind or negative in response to our tenderness, or he or she perceive of our softness as defenselessness, such is not the case at all. In tenderness, we are all powerful. Love is not weak or defenseless. It is the ultimate power!

No one has the ability to offend us if we choose not to take offense. If our love is thrown back in our face or hurtful words are the response from the one we have opened ourselves to, we can choose to deflect the pain by using the very love we feel for that person as a shield. Understand that this person is emotionally unable to accept the gift at this point, respect this present time reality, and release the situation with love. We do not need to stay in a situation where our feelings are not reciprocated or appreciated. Perhaps at a later time, when the other has grown emotionally, the relationship could be renewed.

Often, tenderness melts away resistance and anger in ourselves and invites a similar softening of response in others. Human beings can become defensive at times, hardening their shell in anticipation of an attack from each other. This is especially true if they have experienced unkindness.

When they perceive, instead, tenderness on our part, they realize there is no need for self-defense mechanisms and soften their response as well.

On a personal note:

My husband, Michael, and I went to a non-profit marriage encounter weekend during a period when there was little tenderness to be found between us. So many hurt feelings and disappointments had accumulated that they eclipsed any hope of intimacy. We were focused on each other's shortcomings, and this caused us to be defensive around each other. As we had already experienced one separation, we seemed destined for divorce. We went to this encounter weekend as a last-ditch attempt to salvage our relationship.

During the weekend, we were forced to focus only on each other. Without the kids, dogs and cats, phones, bills, housework, business calls … it was just the two of us. We had both given ourselves the gift of the right environment for tenderness to grow, and were able to focus on just our relationship. We were instructed to write letters to each other … not about the problems which we were having, but on how we felt when we first met. What qualities attracted us to the other person? When did we first realize we were falling in love? How would we feel if the other person died today? What would we miss? Without belittling the other person, we were instructed to write what the other person could do to please us. We were asked to identify the things our spouse did that made us happy. If we had children, we were asked to write how we felt toward each other at the moment of the birth of our first child. As we wrote to each other, it was free of interruption. While writing, no one could interrupt the flow of our thoughts or change the subject. We each got to communicate our thoughts completely. When the writing sessions were over, we were instructed to listen to each other's letters without comment until the last word was read.

As the weekend progressed, I began to feel the resentment and frustration melt away like layers of ice exposed to sunlight. I began to feel hope that through opening up to each other, and exposing our raw hearts, that we could find our way back to each other by allowing tenderness to develop. We each took a chance, and it did not feel comfortable to expose ourselves at first. Through tenderness, we spoke from the heart, and seeds of intimacy and trust were sown.

You have to take the risk, though, and trust that you will be safe regardless of the response of the one you open yourself up to.

Soul play:

+ Be courageous! Invite intimacy into a relationship by talking to someone in your life about setting aside an evening to get together to just talk. (Don't be surprised or discouraged if you get some eye rolling as a response!) Men, traditionally, are less responsive to such a suggestion than women. Don't be deterred, and don't be concerned if there are several attempts before you get a date set.

+ Tenderness and intimacy are necessary components of all relationships: parent-child, sibling-sibling, friend-friend, lover-lover, etc. Don't limit yourself to only exploring tenderness in a relationship with a significant other.

+ Reassure the other person that the "date" is not a gripe session but an occasion to express loving thoughts and feelings for each other.

+ Arrange to have your environment coordinated to avoid interruption. Turn off the phones, have the animals fed and walked, send the kids to Grandma's for the night, turn off the TV, have the house cleaned— anything to reduce distraction.

+ Make up a list of questions with a positive tone to them. If writing down answers is too tedious for one or both of you, agree to allow one another to answer each question fully, without comment, until you have each expressed everything you desire to say.

+ Once both of you have answered your chosen question, comment to each other in a loving, non-judgmental way. This will encourage trust to continue the process.

+ Be understanding if the other person has a difficult time opening up. Do not put undue pressure on him or her as this will just harden his or her shell further. Regardless of another's ability to engage in intimacy, we can still explore the power of tenderness and set a loving example for the other person to follow.

Tolerance

In many ways, tolerance can be a loving, wise, and beneficial choice. By choosing to be tolerant of another's lifestyle, culture, religion, or beliefs, we open up a loving and respectful base for peaceful communication. At the very least, it allows us to "live and let live" and harmoniously follow our separate paths.

Tolerance of our own perceived inadequacies can enable us to feel content with who we are and can thereby promote inner peace and self-acceptance. But, as with many principles, when taken to an extreme, tolerance can become a choice of apathy or avoidance. It can become all too easy to accept the unacceptable, rationalize destructive behaviors, overlook warning signs, or minimize events.

We must guard ourselves against this type of choice by continually examining the results of it. By being tolerant, have we brought more joy and love into the situation? Or have we encouraged incorrect behavior?

There are times when tolerance is appropriate at the beginning of a situation but transitions into destructiveness when we haven't identified when the time is rife to say "enough." Through caring, attentive tolerance we can avoid the pitfalls of apathy. By our conscious attention to the moments of our lives, we can identify warning signals that tell us when our or another's actions have crossed the boundaries of acceptability. If not for this vigilance, it is easy to convince ourselves that incorrect behaviors are "normal." We lose sight of our own values in this way.

The first step in preventing the misuse of tolerance is to become clear in our own values and set boundaries accordingly. When we, or another, act in a way that encroaches upon these boundaries, tolerance needs to take a back seat to respectful but assertive limit setting.

Don't be afraid to "raise the bar" on what we value. We can choose to set our boundaries to limit destructive behavior and thereby lead a happier life. We do not have to accept the status quo just because we have encouraged an unacceptable situation in the past. There is always a choice, in each moment, to decide to say, "Enough!"

On a personal note:

I think it's safe to say that everyone agrees that tolerance is a good thing. I try to practice a good, healthy level of tolerance with my personal relationships. I promote tolerance at work and hope it thrives in our communities. But aside from this definition of tolerance, I felt that this concept—taken to its extreme—was necessary to explore.

I continually have to check myself to see if I am going beyond my own limits, resulting in negative consequences. Who am I kidding? I'm still exploring the concept of defining and setting my own limits! I see the results of failing to raise my standards every time I look in the mirror. But we are all a work in progress and each have our crosses to bear. As I write about this topic, it is causing me to take a good hard look at what my standards are (and aren't). I will be working on the Soul Play right along beside you!

When I was a little girl, I had a friend named Sondra. Sondra was one of ten children in her family. We were ten years old when she confided in me—after much pinky swearing not to tell—that her father did bad things to her. At ten years of age, while we sat on the floor playing with Barbies, my friend told me her father had sex with her. She'd had to explain what sex was to me. There were also beatings. She told me about the time her father held her by the neck against the wall and punched her full fisted in her face. He had broken her nose, leaving it slightly crooked. The scariest part, she said, was seeing splatters of blood on the white walls of her room. She'd had to scrub the wall herself afterward. Her mother never did anything to help her because it was easier to tolerate it than fight it. Sondra grew up and became tolerant to the abuse of her spouse as well, continuing a pattern that ultimately resulted in her death at his hands. This was such a tragic end to an intelligent, sensitive, gentle, and loving young woman, who worried more for her siblings than for herself.

When I was working nights at a healthcare facility, a nursing assistant who worked the day shift came in at 4:30 AM crying and pleading for help. I calmed her down enough to tell me what happened while I cleaned the blood dripping down her arm. Her boyfriend had taken the claw end of a hammer and beat her with it. We called a women's shelter and made arrangements for her to be taken there so that she would be safe. She quit work, and I heard about a year later that she'd gone to back to her boyfriend and was in jail for murder for stabbing him to death.

What would have happened in each of these cases had the victim refused to allow the behaviors to continue? What if Sondra had taken my advice while she was still dating the madman she married, and joined the navy to get away? *What if?* The time to say "Enough!" in an abusive situation is *now*.

Soul play:

+ How has being tolerant been beneficial in your life? Is there someone you know who could benefit from setting aside judgment and allowing him or her the benefit of a live-and-let-live philosophy?

+ Is there a situation in your life where it is time to say "Enough!"? Write down why you should no longer tolerate the situation.

+ Are you allowing yourself, or another, to behave in a hurtful or destructive way? Evaluate why you have allowed this behavior. Do you believe it is "easier" to ignore the behavior rather than deal with it and set limits?

+ Examine and explore how forcing yourself to set appropriate limits, while not the easy route, is ultimately the most beneficial to everyone concerned.

+ If choosing to no longer tolerate destructive behaviors puts you in harm's way, begin to *act* on a plan immediately to remove yourself from the environment. Reach out to others, and the help will be there. By refusing to be abused, you are assisting the growth of the one abusing you. It is the only truly loving choice. An abuser is emotionally or mentally ill and needs help.

+ Sit down and make a list of things you will no longer tolerate. Raise the bar on your values and standards.

+ Decide to be aware, in each moment and with each situation you encounter today, to be vigilant in protecting your raised standards. People, even your own subconscious, will object at first. They will ultimately begin to come around, as long as you persist.

Trust

Trust is the giving over of one's life, and the outcomes of one's experiences, to the Source with the understanding that whatever occurs will ultimately serve our soul's purpose. We do not bring with us into this earthly excursion the remembrance of the various lessons we chose to learn or the experiences we chose to live. Nor do we remember the purposes behind choosing them. We knowingly accepted this veil over our spiritual eyes.

The reason this veil exists is to provide us the forgetting we required to enable us to experience being separate from God. How can we fully appreciate being part of something so magnificent and perfect unless we have first experienced its opposite? Unless we separate ourselves from it, we have no frame of reference. How can we understand and appreciate light without having experienced darkness?

Because this veil allows us this experience of separateness, it is easy for us to forget that we are part of the Source. For those of us who do not realize our connection to each other and to this Source, life often feels like being in a raft ... without paddles ... sitting in the middle of the ocean getting tossed around by the waves. This creates feelings of helplessness, hopelessness, and worry.

Trusting is necessary to overcome these disempowering emotions. Trust that not only are we in the raft, but we are the raft ... and the paddles ... and the ocean. We have created our own waves. The separateness is merely a paradigm.

When we understand that we have created the storms of our lives and can trust that we will be okay regardless of outcomes, we will cease our worrying. This is not to say we will not experience pain or sadness. It is necessary that we do. But trust enables us to do this without worry, without feelings of helplessness, and without the sting of bitterness.

Trusting serves another purpose as well. When we send out our intentions to manifest something in our lives, if we fuss and worry, we are sending the universe the wrong message. We are, in effect, saying "I doubt," and this will not assist us in achieving our goals. By sending out a message of trust instead, we are drawing positive energy toward us.

On a personal note:

As usual, when I am about to write about a topic I get to experience something relevant. In this case, the universe couldn't have thrown me a better example. I've been having trouble swallowing, and it's gotten worse lately. I tried to get a vitamin down a few days ago, and it took me a half hour to unclog it and pass it through with about a half gallon of water. I'd told the doctor about it before, and she hadn't been very concerned. But this new development seemed to cause quite a bit of concern, and I am now awaiting my appointment with a specialist, who will conduct multiple tests.

As a nurse, I am aware of the diagnosis this symptom could signify. My own father-in-law has been struggling with esophageal cancer for several years. I am fully aware that I could face the same battle. My first reaction to this possibility was fear. Fear of future pain, financial instability, and of how my family would manage without me. Then came feelings of regret … regret I hadn't finished this book … that I didn't spend more quality time with my family … that I spent too much time on paperwork instead of with my patients … and regret that I may have missed opportunities to demonstrate love and kindness. I wish I had spent more time doing the things I love and less time pursuing unproductive recreation and mindlessly watching reruns on TV.

When I sat down to write this morning, I was feeling the fear and regret … like a bad dream that didn't end when I woke up. I chose this topic because I needed to remember how important trust was in this outcome. I remember now that I will be okay even if I do have cancer … my ultimate outcome is assured. Whether it is cancer or not, I am grateful for having had this experience. It has made me more aware of where the focus of my life needs to be. I don't want to regret what I haven't done.

I know there is a greater plan directing my path, and I know I was directly involved in the creation of this plan. I trust that whatever happens will be exactly as intended, and I will try to align my responses with my higher self and let the ocean take me where it will.

Soul play:

+ Which area of your life do you worry over? How does worrying about it create feelings of helplessness? How does worrying send out a lack of trust?

+ Has there been an experience in your life that has been painful, or caused you to feel that life is unfair, or that the universe is conspiring against you?

+ How can trusting that, on a soul level, this event was necessary help you look for a deeper meaning for the experience?

+ How can knowing you were directly involved in the planning of the event in your life make you feel more empowered?

Understanding

Understanding is gaining full knowledge of an issue, event, opinion, and so on. It is neither agreeing nor disagreeing with someone else's perspective.

To come into an understanding of something, we must set aside emotionality and look at the issue from all sides and observe other people's reactions and perceptions without judgment. To understand, judgment needs to be set aside. Understanding is simply an observation of what is.

In order to understand, gather as much information as possible. Ask the questions: who, what, where, and when. Determine any feelings involved. Again, withhold judgment. We are seeking, at this point, only to understand.

Before we decide which perspective or feelings we have regarding an issue, we must first understand it fully. Listening skills are required here. What good does formulating questions do if we are unable or unwilling to listen to the answers?

Why is it important to seek understanding? Because in order to choose a response that best serves our highest vision of ourselves and others, we must first understand every aspect of the issue at hand. Also, deliberate evaluation, armed with a determination to suspend judgment, buys us time to avoid an immediate feeling-based response that may not reflect our higher selves.

When we make the effort to understand, we demonstrate respect for another's right to choose his or her own perspective and open lines for greater communication. Each of us yearns for the respect of being understood, even if others do not agree with us.

On a personal note:

It is easy to become so caught up in our own views of things that we miss the bigger picture because of a lack of understanding. How many times have we reacted to a particular event out of hurt or frustration, and later (many nasty words later) come to find that the other involved never meant to hurt our feelings or upset us?

When we react with that knee-jerk response and forget to initiate the process of "understanding" a situation, we are setting ourselves up to put our foot in our mouth! And I for one have had my share of tasting shoe leather! So what can we do to avoid having to eat our own words? We need to use our words to ask questions instead of make comments.

If we ask another person "what" he or she meant by a comment we have taken offense to, we might discover that it was something totally innocent . If we ask "who" the other person was referring to, we might discover the other was not speaking in reference to us. If we ask "how" the other person came to a particular conclusion, we might be able to clarify a misunderstanding on his or her part. If we ask "when," we might discover that something occurred during a very stressful time in the other person's life, when he or she was weak or vulnerable, which resulted in his or her current viewpoint.

Conscious awareness is necessary in any attempt to change our habits. Seeking to understand as a first response to encountering ideas or views that differ from our own is a habit! It does not come to us naturally! We have to work toward ingraining this response through conscious effort. As it is with learning all new skills, be patient with yourself. There will be times when we will blow it, and out will come our opinionated voice before we can effectively shut it up long enough to listen. That's okay, though, because it's all part of the process of evolution. We are evolving our responses to reflect the highest vision we can imagine in ourselves.

Our higher self is always aware of the most loving response, but our everyday self becomes distracted by the day-to-day chaos of our lives. It is easy to forget to stop and tap into our higher consciousness. The higher self is aware that every moment, every reaction, is a choice with consequences. It holds the wisdom to direct the process. By taking a breath before jumping to inaccurate conclusions or speculations, we would be wise to consult our higher self and seek understanding.

The more we practice stepping back from our reactions and look to understand a situation from all sides, the easier such an undertaking becomes. It does not come automatically ... it takes work. But the reward is that we become a closer resemblance to our highest vision of ourselves.

Soul play:

+ Make a conscious choice that on this very day you will endeavor to understand a viewpoint or opinion that differs from your own. You will seek out such an opposition to your beliefs and learn all you can about it.

+ Compose a list of questions that will help you understand the opposing viewpoint better. Incorporate the "who, what, where, and when" method.

+ Avoid making comments while undertaking the process of understanding. It is safer to stick with questions. The questions should not be leading (so as to convince another of your own viewpoint), nor should they be sarcastic.

+ Ask your higher self to participate and assist you in developing a full understanding of the situation, and allow your innate wisdom to express itself.

+ Remember that understanding has nothing to do with agreeing with another's position. Be prepared, however, to accept that your own viewpoint may shift into a clearer view when you fully understand a situation from all sides.

+ Expect to make mistakes when learning this skill, and be patient with yourself. The rewards are well worth your diligence.

Willingness

Willingness is the overcoming of our ego's tendency to only be concerned with self. It is reaching out instead, to serve another without complaint and without coercion.

Willingness requires not only that we assist when we are asked. There are countless people in need of spiritual, physical, or emotional assistance, but often they are too shy, afraid, or embarrassed to ask for help. Sometimes we walk around with blinders on, oblivious to the plight of others. When we are willing, we take the blinders off and can then see the hurt and pain in another's eyes.

When we serve to lessen the burden of others, we are (on a spiritual level) lightening our own load. We are all one on this spiritual level, living separate existences. To uplift one is to uplift all. This is why, when we willingly serve another, we are rewarded with a sense of satisfaction, fulfillment, and joy.

When we make the decision to become willing participants, ready to serve with loving heart and hands, we are gifted with the energy of the Source. Suddenly, new ideas flow that help us accomplish the tasks at hand. Insights come quickly, and the work is performed smoothly and efficiently. This is especially evident when many are gathered with the purpose of service, because the energy is multiplied.

There are times we are in an emotional and spiritual slump and may not be in a position to willingly serve. When we contemplate the prospect of service to another resentfully, we can actually create more disharmony and negativity by participating. If we are angry because we feel forced or coerced into helping, we may take our frustration out on the very ones who need our assistance. To do so is detrimental and unnecessary. If such is the case, refrain from helping. It is more productive and less disruptive to be honest with ourselves about our reluctance to serve. We should honor our own feelings. When we feel this reluctance, we should ask ourselves why. More often than not, when we don't want to help another, we are need of uplifting and nurturing ourselves. This is when we must fill our own cup so that we might be able at some point to assist others.

Ironically, it is often through serving another and losing focus on our own ego's hurts that we become uplifted and nourished. Sometimes if we set aside our resentment and serve "as if" we are happy to do it, we step into generosity of heart. There is no greater balm to our own hurts than getting our minds off ourselves and helping someone else feel better.

On a personal note:

My favorite TV show is *Extreme Home Makeover*. It's like *Touched by an Angel*, only in a reality-TV format. The angels in this show are real life, and the people they touch are in need of a loving hand. These people are coping with a myriad of difficulties, ranging from a widower with eight beautiful children (and a little house), to trying to provide a somewhat normal life to a child allergic to the sun. As we get to know these families, we want to see them happy. The crew building these incredibly inspirational homes work together with volunteers, friends, and neighbors to build these houses and enrich the lives of those who will live in it. When you see everyone working together, with a full spirit of willingness and joy to help, the energy is palpable! Just watching the show is such a rush. I can only imagine what the crew must feel like knowing they were responsible for bringing such happiness into the lives of these deserving families.

When my children were very young, and I wasn't working full-time, I had some opportunities to volunteer to go food shopping for an elderly couple. They were in their 90s, and it was just too hard for them to manage on their own, but they just couldn't leave their home to go into a nursing facility. There were days I wanted to do just about anything other than shop for another household with three small kids in tow! But when I thought about what this small service meant to this couple, I set aside my wants and put on my as-if frame of mind and served with a smile. When I went about the business of picking out the best fruit for them (I've never known people to eat so healthy! No wonder they lived so long!), as long as I got into the spirit of service, the kids and I had a good time, and I was teaching them an important principle.

Each time we brought those carefully chosen groceries to this couple, their eyes lit up with happiness, and they were so grateful that someone had taken the time to care. Of course, I would feel guilty for starting out preferring to watch a talk show on TV, but the end result was very much worth the effort it took.

One year, my whole family adopted a single mom and her three kids at Christmas. Everybody bought toys, clothes, games, toiletries, the makings for a full turkey dinner (complete with pumpkin and apple pies and a bottle of Champaign for the mom). I felt like Santa Claus carrying those bags up her steps. When I was joyously, but shyly, invited in, I felt a mixture of feelings—sadness that there were no presents under their little tree, and satisfaction that, as I emptied the bounty in those bags, there would be tons of great presents for everyone. I was aware of how self-conscious this single mom felt and lost no time telling her how happy she'd made my family to have been able to do this for her. I reassured her that we all felt blessed for the opportunity and hugged her before leaving, and there were tears of gratitude in both of our eyes.

Soul play:

+ Rather than calling out, "Hi, how are you?" as you rush past people, take a moment to wait for the answer. Make eye contact and give your full attention to the verbal and non-verbal answers.
+ If you observe pain or distress in the response, commit to being willing to offer assistance, even if it is just to listen. Sometimes just listening with a sympathetic ear or offering a smile and word of encouragement is all that is needed to uplift someone. Monitor your response to a plea for help. Be honest! Do you feel pressured or resentful? Evaluate why you feel this way. What healing or nourishment do you feel in need of? How can you be more nurturing to yourself?
+ Try an experiment. If you feel you're in a slump and are feeling sorry for yourself, or you feel empty of the desire to help someone else, dive headfirst into the service of another! Try looking for a group project, as there is tremendous energy to feed your soul while you are actively engaged in serving others. Group service projects have abounding healing energy. Just be prepared to put on your as-if frame of mind so you don't bring everyone else down before they have the chance to uplift you!

Breinigsville, PA USA
29 March 2011
258638BV00001B/3/P